D1645427

THE MIND OF MAN

       I have felt
A presence that disturbs me with the joy
Of elevated thoughts; a sense sublime
Of something far more deeply interfused,
Whose dwelling is the light of setting suns,
And the round ocean and the living air,
And the blue sky, and in the mind of man :
A motion and a spirit, that impels
All thinking things, all objects of all thought,
And rolls through all things.

    WORDSWORTH : *Lines composed a few miles
        above Tintern Abbey*

THE MIND OF MAN

GILBERT HIGHET

Geoffrey Cumberlege

OXFORD UNIVERSITY PRESS

London   New York   Toronto

1954

Oxford University Press, Amen House, London E.C.4

GLASGOW   NEW   YORK   TORONTO   MELBOURNE   WELLINGTON
BOMBAY   CALCUTTA   MADRAS   KARACHI   CAPE   TOWN   IBADAN

Geoffrey Cumberlege, Publisher to the University

PRINTED IN GREAT BRITAIN

CONTENTS

INTRODUCTION

THIS book contains two meditations on the human mind —its powers and limitations, its growth, and its destinies. The first of these studies, *Man's Unconquerable Mind,* is philosophical; the second, *The Migration of Ideas,* is historical. Together, they are the product of some twenty years of reflection: beginning, I suppose, in 1933, when I first read Spengler's *Decline of the West* and attempted to detect the gaps in his powerful but inadequate theory of history; continuing through the years when I translated Werner Jaeger's wonderfully stimulating book on the educational significance of Greek civilization, *Paideia*[1]; reaching a further stage with my introduction to Toynbee's *Study of History;* continuing to develop later, when, during five years cut off from academic life, I endeavoured to understand the astonishing confusion of highly intelligent planning and irrational, almost insane, passions which accompanied the second world war; then resuming in 1946, when I began to describe one aspect of the strange link between the modern world and the civilization of Greece and Rome, in *The Classical Tradition,*[2] and in 1950, when in *The Art of Teaching,*[3] I discussed one of the essential relationships between different minds.

These two studies were written down at the same time, but they were worked out in different ways.

The Migration of Ideas presents a neglected conception of history. It suggests that, as well as describing the shifts of

[1] Blackwell, Oxford, three volumes, 1939, 1943, 1944.

[2] Clarendon Press, Oxford, 1949.

[3] Methuen, London, 1951.

political power and the workings of economic conflict and co-operation, historians ought also to expound the influence of ideas on human affairs—particularly the influence of ideas moving from one group, nation, or culture into another and fertilizing it. I first put out this suggestion in a single lecture to the Graduate History Society of Columbia University; then later, as the conception developed and illustrations accumulated, in groups of lectures delivered elsewhere; and finally in March, 1954 as the North Foundation Lectures at Franklin and Marshall College, Lancaster, Pennsylvania. My gratitude is due to all the institutions which gave me hospitality and a sympathetic hearing, and to the foundations which sponsored the delivery of the lectures at various stages: in particular, to the University of Kansas; to the United States Military Academy at West Point; to Emory University and its Walter Turner Candler Lectureship; to Hamilton College and its Winslow Lectureship; and finally to the North Foundation, the Trustees, and the staff of Franklin and Marshall College.

The Migration of Ideas is, so to speak, the result of many discussions held with audiences interested in the meaning of history. *Man's Unconquerable Mind* grew out of a long debate with myself. The year 1954 marked the 200th anniversary of the foundation of King's College, Columbia University, where I have the honour to teach. The University chose, as the theme which best expressed its past history and its future duties, the concept *Man's Right to Knowledge and the Free Use Thereof.* Either this is an inspiring but vague copybook maxim, or it is a serious concept involving problems that need thoughtful examination. Has every man and woman the right to full knowledge of all subjects? Even if they have, can they possibly attain such knowledge? If they can, how should they use it? Do they even wish to possess it? And what, both in education and in life, is the real relation between the human reason and the other activities of mankind? *Man's Unconquerable Mind* was written as a study of these and other questions implicit in the Columbia Bicentennial theme, and indeed in the work of scholarship and teaching wherever it is carried on.

I am grateful to the authors and publishers of the books cited in the notes and bibliographies, and to the firms that have permitted me to quote passages from works in which they hold copyright: Messrs. Faber and Faber, from the poems of T. S. Eliot and Stephen Spender; Messrs. Macmillan and Co. Ltd., from the poetry of Ralph Hodgson; William Heinemann Ltd., from *Odtaa,* by John Masefield; and Messrs. Harcourt, Brace, & Co., from *Hitler's Secret Conversations,* edited by H. R. Trevor-Roper (published in England as *Hitler's Table Talk,* by Weidenfeld & Nicolson.)

A little earlier, I said that the thoughts which produced this book began in 1933, with my first reading of Oswald Spengler. But it would be truer to say that they began in 1929, when, with much pride and much humility, I entered Balliol College: for it was there that I first, in the conversation and companionship of Cyril Bailey, felt the inexplicable power of a wise teacher, and, in the studies, lecture-rooms, and libraries of Oxford University, began to realize something of the lasting happiness of the life of the mind.

Columbia University, New York.   G.H.
March, 1954.

MAN'S UNCONQUERABLE MIND

Thou hast left behind
Powers that will work for thee; air, earth, and skies;
There's not a breathing of the common wind
That will forget thee; thou hast great allies;
Thy friends are exultations, agonies,
And love, and man's unconquerable mind.

WORDSWORTH : *To Toussaint L'Ouverture*

CHAPTER ONE

Wonders are Many

IN one of the noblest of Greek tragedies, a young girl learns
that the body of her brother—denounced as a rebel and
traitor—has been left in a desert place to rot, or to be
eaten by wolves and vultures. On pain of death the government has forbidden anyone to bury the corpse. After terrible
heart-searching, the girl determines that it is her duty to
break this law, although it means sacrificing her happiness
and her life. Her own sister refuses to go with her, weeps,
and tries to dissuade her. But she moves away toward her
heroic and terrible destiny.

Soon after, a breathless sentry rushes in, to report that, in
spite of the new official order and in spite of the heavy guard
on the corpse, someone has visited it and performed the rites
of burial. The autocratic ruler of the country, infuriated by
this outrage against authority, commands that the whole
area shall be searched and the criminal arrested for immediate punishment. A group of citizens hears the news with
astonishment—with awe; and then breaks out into a song
of solemn and heartfelt admiration for the incalculable
ingenuity of human beings.

> Wonders are many, but none,
>   none is more wondrous than man.
> Man moves over the grey sea,
>   using the wind and the storm,
>   daring the depths and surges.

Even the eldest of all the gods—
    Earth, inexhaustible Earth—
man masters her
    with yearly ploughs that turn and return
    and the steady step of the horse.
Language and thought
    light and rapid as wind,
man has taught himself these, and has learnt
    the ways of living in town and city,
    shelter from inhospitable frost,
    escape from the arrows of rain.
Cunning, cunning is man.

Wise though his plans are,
    artful beyond all dreaming,
they carry him both to evil and to good.

The chorus might have sung a hymn to destiny, the cruel providence that seems to pass over certain men and women while it selects others for agonizing conflicts and mortal decisions; or to heroism, the invisible iron in the blood that makes some of those who suffer rise above pity into admiration and honour. Instead, it praises the thinking mind—which, together with a myriad other activities, contains the will; and which can transcend destiny not only through defying it but through understanding it.

This hymn to the mind of man is itself a marvellous product of mind. The poet Sophocles took one part of a remote prehistoric legend which had come down to him over unimaginable gulfs of darkness, the death of the princess Antigone, daughter of the tormented king Oedipus. He divined its eternal meaning. He grouped its actions and its characters into the severe harmonies of that new and magnificent invention, the tragic drama. He gave them speech:

the winning, subtle, and powerful words of the Greek tongue, one of the most exquisite instruments ever devised by human beings. To carry still more delicate and penetrating meanings, he transformed all their speech into poetry, so that his creatures uttered their thoughts (his thoughts) in the strong, steady, but flexible rhythm of dramatic verse—another recent invention of the Greeks, which later peoples have adopted without surpassing—and the chorus voiced their emotions of pity, fear, and amazement in the more fluid pulse of a song which was at the same time a dance. Sophocles composed music for his play, and devised ceremonious dances for his choir: we cannot see the dance now, nor hear the music, but we may sense them both in the beat and the melody of his words. And he is dead, and his actors are dead, and all those who saw and heard the tragedy of Antigone played in Athens twenty-four centuries ago have vanished. The theatre is a heap of ruins. The very language which he used has long since left the tongues of mankind.

Yet the words and the thoughts of Sophocles do not die. Men learn, with vast difficulty and yet with admiration, to read the words. They study the subtle construction of the play. With their inward ear they reanimate the rhythms and the harmonies of the verse. They hear the very voices of the characters, proud heroine and inflexible lawgiver. They marvel at that inexhaustible miracle, the human mind: which can think such thoughts, give them such superb shape, and then, over enormous changes in language and history and belief, transmit them to be re-thought and to create new thoughts in other minds. And, as they read, they are once more aware of the meaning of the tragedy: which is that men and women must think, and must feel themselves free to think; that the lowest misery is slavery, not of the body, but of thought; and that even when our life is harsh and inexplicable, we may still make it into a worthy and heroic destiny, provided we maintain the invincibility of the mind.

CHAPTER TWO

Homo Sapiens

THINKING. Learning, remembering, knowing, imagining and creating new ideas; preserving and communicating knowedge over distances in time and space. Not only is it wonderful in its compass and variety: it is unique. It makes us human.

ANIMALS OR MEN

Consider our lives. All other activities we share with the other inhabitants of the planet. Animals, birds, reptiles, fish, and insects also struggle for power, as we do. They organize themselves into social groups. Many build. Some control their environment by ingenious inventions. Some of them, like some of us, collect wealth. They fight. They make love. They play games. Some have powers we shall never possess and can scarcely comprehend. Cunning and skilful, that they are. Yet collectively they learn little that is new, and individually almost nothing. Their skills are intricate, but limited. Their art, though charming, is purely decorative. Their languages consist of a few dozen signs and sounds. Their memory is vivid but restricted. Their curiosity is shallow and temporary, merely the rudiment of that wonder which fills the mind of a human scientist or poet or historian or philosopher. They cannot conceive of learning and knowledge as a limitless activity administered by the power of will. Only human beings really learn, and know, and remember, and think creatively as individuals far beyond the limitations of any single group or the dominance of any single need. Knowledge acquired and extended for its own sake is the specific quality that makes us human. Our species has the hair and lungs of animals, reptilian bones, and fish-like blood. We are close indeed to the beasts; often we are more cruel. But we are fundamentally different from them in that we can learn almost infinitely, and know, and recollect. We are *Homo sapiens:* Man the Thinker.

The life of every individual man and woman is made up of many acts and passions. But it is most clearly and consistently seen as a pattern of learning. We think all the time. Our thoughts and our experiences continually form a mass of material which we accept and try to organize. It is chiefly in the depth and completeness of its organization that we differ from one another.

We all recognize this: it is a familiar notion. But it is a less familiar concept that all human history—with all its multitudinous glories and disgraces and crimes and heroisms —might be best understood as a process of learning. The process is troubled, delayed, interrupted, reversed sometimes, and sometimes arrested for long periods. Yet it is always traceable, and when in forward movement always admirable.

History as the record of struggles for power is exciting but unrewarding. Dinosaurs tore at one another for ages: some survived; some died: it is all meaningless. Tribes of human beings have been hunting and rending and enslaving one another for many centuries. This one had the longer claws, that had the stouter muscles, another hid in ambush. It is factual, but is it important? Does it even explain the spread of mankind over the face of the planet, or is it merely a side activity? No: surely our real, our essential history is the story of our learning and thinking.

It was by learning that we ceased to be animals and made ourselves into men. That was the first stage. It was then, far back in the warm jungles, that somehow, cell by cell and reflex by reflex, the wonderful human brain was formed, and with it our two other human powers—the devices by which, even if the world fell into ruins, we could still rebuild it—our fantastically intricate speech, and our ingenious adaptable hands.

TOOLS

And then, still far back in the darkness of forest and cave, we learned how to use tools. Even better, we learned how to make tools. Prehistoric archaeology is a discipline in which there is much guesswork. But one thing in it is certain, and contains much pathos and much charm: the slow and impressive advance of our distant selves from animalism to humanity, learning, learning, always learning. In any good museum there will be a case full of prehistoric stone tools—hammers, axes, or scrapers—arranged in series. The earliest are scarcely more than lumps of stone, with a few corners chipped off to fit the rough hand roughly. But to gaze at them, those tools of the brutish dawn-men, and then to examine the rest of the series, to see how, very gradually, slow century by century, better stones are selected, and their heft and balance are studied, and instead of being crudely pounded into edged lumps, they are sliced and chipped and flaked and smoothed and rounded and sharpened and polished until they are not only efficient but

almost handsome; and then to imagine those remote ancestors working away at them, thinking or learning to think,
talking or learning to talk, while they worked, so that the
urgent simple need of having a flint fit to kill a wolf
developed into the pleasure of possessing an instrument well
made for its own sake and even decorative, and the habit
of improvisation grew into a craft and a tradition, and the
growth of refinement created new powers, needs, hopes, and
rituals—ah, it is impossible to look at those stone tools and
to imagine their makers without feeling pity, admiration,
and affection for our clever industrious ancestors, without
seeing them as part of the same series of makers and inventors to which we ourselves belong, and without renewing
our reverence for the growth of the human mind.

This is real history, the record of such a growth. After the
stone tools came other inventions: the control of fire; the
skilful, almost magical transformation of lumps of earth
into hard pottery and durable metal; the creation of the
wheels which have ever since been rolling across the face
of the earth. And at some long-distant time clever men also
invented animal helpers. That is, they took wild creatures—
the horses and buffaloes and pigs which they had once
hunted and eaten, the wolves they had once fought, the
jungle and swamp fowl they had once shot and trapped—
and trained them slowly, generation by generation, to live
patiently and even willingly in the company of men. It is
strange to watch a puppy in a kennel, whining and scratch-
ing at the door, eager for the companionship of any human
being, and to reflect on the long centuries it took to tame
his ancestors, the captured whelps reared with the tough
cave-children (reversing the tale of Mowgli and the wolf-
cubs), playing and feeding and wrestling and sleeping beside

the common fire, and then running down the same prey, tearing at the same warm meat and cracking the white bones together, until they became, as they now are, fast friends of man rather than servants. (When the American continent was discovered in 1492, it had millions of inhabitants at many different stages of civilization. They had tame dogs, but no horses; stone tools and soft-metal products, but no iron; no ploughs; and no wheels. Therefore their ancestors had discovered America and moved into it after dogs and stone tools and pottery were invented, but before the invention of horses, wheels, ploughs, and ironworking.)

PLANTS

Equally wonderful, perhaps more wonderful, was the invention of plants. Almost everything we consume, except animal food, is part of a plant, carefully bred from selected stock: our wheat and sugar, our fruit and roots, the tobacco we smoke, the hemp and cotton we weave—all these and many more were once wild plants growing in the jungle. Some intelligent man or woman found each one of them, tasted or tested it, by patient experiment discovered how to rear it, improved it, fertilized and crossbred it, and thus invented it as surely as Diesel invented his air-fuel-compression-ignition engine. Their names are lost, those inventors, unless they are hidden under Dionysus and Demeter and Hiawatha, for long revered as the gods who taught mankind how to use plants. Yet the studies of modern botanists and archaeologists have told us where they worked. Most of the cultivated plants on earth were developed in a very few regions. Most, by far the most, came from the uplands of western China; next most from India; the next most copious groups came from the East Indies; then from the high plains of central Asia, where our wheat was born; then from Asia Minor, home of orchards (and what else was Eden?); next from the Mediterranean area; lastly from Central America, the Andean highlands, and the Amazon basin, that mysterious and fertile region where, within our own generation, an inventor found a poison, curare, and transformed it into a powerful agent of healing.

That was one of the real beginnings of civilization. In that slow patient process, the men improved the plants, and the plants improved the men. They ceased to live at random. They settled down, and grew together. The First Families were founded, with the well-known names: Mr. Farmer, Mr. Miller, Mr. Gardener, and not far away Mr. Weaver, Mr. Potter, Mr. Carpenter, and the mysterious Mr. Smith. (Mr. Hunter lived some way off in the woods; and the hut on the river-bank was the residence of the Fisher family.) Ploughing came in. The land was improved by clearing and draining. The complex craft of irrigation was discovered, a skill which we are still working to develop. Farms and fisheries and crafts, they soon make a market; a market makes a village, and villages grow into towns, towns into cities. Cultivated fields and systematic irrigation make men invent rules and observe seasons: therefore laws were devised, the calendar was established, and astronomy became both a religion and a science.

So it was through learning, through expanding our knowledge, that we moved from primitive animalism to primitive human savagery, and from savagery to civilization. People sometimes say nowadays that the next war will mean 'the end of civilization'. It might well mean the end of an era in civilization. We, or our surviving remnants, and our descendants, might go savage again for a time. But as long as the planet is livable and as long as we possess, unimpaired, this fifty-ounce organ of exploration and invention and adaptation, the brain, we shall not only be able to reconstruct civilization. We shall be compelled to reconstruct civilization

CHAPTER THREE

Civilization and Thought

ALL important cultures have ingenuities of their own. They are all marvellous manifestations of the power of the mind. But our own culture—western civilization—is the most intellectual of all. More than the others, it is the product of systematic thought. The whole world uses its inventions. Its scientific methods, its educational ideals, its cult of literacy, have been adopted by other civilizations and are transforming them.

Now, the history of western civilization through the last three thousand years—for all its sins and stupidities—can best be understood as a record of the adventures of the thinking mind. Gibbon, who said history was 'little more than the register of the crimes, follies, and misfortunes of mankind', lacked both the temperament and the wisdom to appreciate the continuous activity of legal, religious, and philosophical thought, political experience and experiment, and aesthetic and educational innovation, which alone made his history of the declining Roman empire worth writing And he seems scarcely to have considered the many centuries of magnificent achievement that went before the establishment of the empire. He was an industrious and sonorous stylist, but he had a shallow and superficial mind. Crimes and follies are common to all societies. The drunken chieftain, the perverted scientist, the cruel priest, the stupid soldier—they flourish from east to west and north to south, they appear in kraals and palaces, they existed in the palaeolithic age and will still exist in the atomic age. But the specific difference which has made and maintains our culture is thought.

Those who are most easily depressed about the precarious future of western civilization are usually people who do not know the full history of its past. They also very generally misunderstand our relation to the Greeks and the Romans. They imagine them as remote peoples whose lives and achievements interest antiquarians alone, and whose languages and thoughts are 'dead'. Certainly they always conceive the Greeks and Romans as being more primitive than ourselves, instead of being in many ways more mature and more advanced in knowledge and experience. This is like considering Beethoven backward in comparison with a modern musician because he did not own a hearing aid. In fact, such mistakes are usually caused by a crude belief in Progress as a movement continuous throughout history, virtually automatic, and expressed chiefly in mechanical inventions.

Progress has not been continuous through the last three thousand years of our history—nor the last three hundred; nor even the last thirty. Progress is not a line leading up-wards to infinity. It is a double curve broken by a huge disaster. Each peak of the curve represents a great success of western civilization. Each has lower peaks and shoulders ascending to it. But the two peaks are on almost the same level; and we, who stand lower than the Greeks and Romans in some things and higher in others, can and should look toward them constantly, in order to interpret our own destinies.

THE GREEKS

Our story begins soon after 1000 B.C. with the Greeks. There were other civilizations long before them and contemporary with them, far richer and grander; but only the Greeks *thought*, thought hard and constantly, and thought principally in human terms. They saw themselves as surrounded on all sides by 'barbarians'—which for them meant people who did not live reasonably: eccentrics such as the Egyptians who spent millions on preserving dead bodies, powerful brutes like the Assyrians who worshipped gods that were half-animal, primitive wanderers who could not read or write and had to carry weapons everywhere, devoted ritualists like the Jews, slavish hordes like the subjects of Persia. We imagine the Greeks as cheerful, tranquil people, happily balanced. But perhaps Nietzsche was right in saying that they felt a constant and terrible pressure of barbarism, not only from around them but from within; and that their civilization was not an effortless growth, but the product of courageous effort sustained by acute tension. They must often have felt like a few sane men living in a world of maniacs and constantly endangered by the infection of madness.

Still oftener, however, they felt like mature men surrounded by undeveloped minds, some of whom, though barbarous, would learn. The Greeks drew no colour line.

They had no racial, social, or national barriers around their culture. Any 'barbarian' could enter it if he learnt to speak the language, to behave civilly, and to think. Many of those whom we consider characteristically and intensely Greek came from distant lands and were immigrants to the language and the civilization. That is part of the importance of St. Paul, that though born and bred a Jew he abandoned the rituals of Judaism and Jewish exclusiveness, and set out to preach the universal religion through the Greco-Roman world in the international language, Greek.

In most things of the mind, the Greeks were not only the teachers of their own contemporaries—Jews and Parthians, Romans and Egyptians, wandering barbarians and distant Indians. They were the teachers of all those who followed them in the civilization of the West, down to the present day. They are our teachers, and the teachers of our children. It is not possible for us to deny that powerful influence. It is possible to ignore it only at the risk of thinning and weakening our own minds, of emptying our spiritual homes and bringing in wilder, more foolish spirits to live there.

A great modern scholar has summed up the influence of the Greeks in a single word, and described it in three massive volumes. The scholar is Werner Jaeger, formerly of Berlin and now of Harvard. The word is *paideia*. The book is called *Paideia: The Ideals of Greek Culture*. Originally written in German, it has been translated into many languages, and its guiding concept has been accepted by many thoughtful students of intellectual history. Put very briefly, the concept is this.

Paideia in Greek means education (it is the same word we see in encyclopaedia); but it also means civilization—culture, in the highest sense. This is because the Greeks believed that all civilization and all progress were based on education, lifelong education, enjoyment and improvement of all the highest powers of the mind. Other nations have held that their own civilization meant power—or service to God—or service to the divine monarch—or wealth and comfort. Several nations in our own day sometimes seem to believe that if everyone had plenty to eat and drink and owned a motorcar and a few other machines, life would be perfect. The Greeks too enjoyed life with all its delights, wine, women, and song, sports and dancing: many of them gave up their whole existence to light pleasures; but, centrally, they knew what was better, and their greatest men pursued and maintained it. This was quite simply the improvement of the mind. It was in order to help men to think that their great poets composed, their philosophers and historians wrote, their orators spoke. They were teachers, Homer, Aeschylus, Aristophanes; Thucydides, Plato, Aristotle; Pindar, Simonides, Menander: these and many more were, first and foremost, doctors of the soul.

This of course is why we still must read their works. We read them not because they are 'historic', but because they teach us, they make us think. Nowhere else in the entire literature of the world, in any language or any single period, is there such a rich, varied, and deeply thoughtful collection of books as those produced by the Greeks and their successors, the Romans. The central purpose of studying the Greek and Latin languages is to read these books in the original: all other purposes are subsidiary or specialist. Translations are not good enough—partly because there are so few good translators and partly because English is a poorer, weaker language than Greek, and has so far been less subtly developed than Latin.

Western readers, Christian and Jewish, will at once think of those other collections of books produced by the Jewish genius and known (through a mistranslation) as the Old and New Testaments. If it is permissible to compare the books of the Bible with the books of Greece and Rome, then there are two important distinctions which we must make. One is that the style of the Bible is vastly simpler and more monotonous, and that its books pay far less attention to logical and aesthetic structure. The other is that the Bible largely depends on authority and revelation. Its precepts come from the God of the universe, through different media or mediators. The Greeks and their Roman successors do not appeal to divine authority. The Voice they listen to is the utterance, not of superhuman power, but of reason calmly discussing what is, what has been, and what should be. A wise man of our own time was once asked what was the single greatest contribution of Greece to the world's welfare. He replied 'The greatest invention of the Greeks was $\mu\acute{\epsilon}\nu$ and $\delta\acute{\epsilon}$'. For $\mu\acute{\epsilon}\nu$ means 'on the one hand', and $\delta\acute{\epsilon}$ means 'on the other hand'. Without these two balances, we cannot think.

The Greeks therefore taught one another, by thinking, and talking, and writing. And then they taught the rest of the western world. One of the chief pleasures of studying aesthetic and intellectual history is to see how their ideas —or rather the ideas of Reason which found voice in them —reappear in distant times, through complex transitions, among men who know little directly of Greek. It is one of the central proofs of the power of the free-ranging mind. If we open Dante's *Comedy* and watch the poet in his vision descending through Hell—a Hell divided into three main regions, for the punishment of Incontinence, Violence, and

Deceit—we recognize the moral system of the Greek philosopher Aristotle. If we see Shakespeare's *Macbeth*, we reflect that the form of the tragedy and its basic sense were both created by the poets of Greece. The balance of powers on which the American constitution rests was first formulated by a Greek historical thinker, and Greek teachers first stated that lofty ideal, the brotherhood of man.

GREEKS AND ROMANS

The first pupils of the Greeks were the Romans: an unpromising set. When they first saw the Romans they called them 'barbarians', and believed them determined but dull. It was not through Greek art that Rome conquered and administered the western world, and perhaps, like some modern empires, she might have remained barbarous and crude even after becoming rich and powerful. But instead, the Romans humbled themselves in the midst of their conquest, and set about learning from the Greeks. They had no literature of permanent value. They had no sciences. They could not reason philosophically. Even their language, though forcible and flexible, was clumsy. In all these fields the Greeks taught them, and, like good teachers, elicited qualities they themselves scarcely possessed. The result was another flowering of Greek culture transplanted to Italy— or rather, more truly, the creation of a new joint culture, the Greco-Roman civilization, in which the two elements are often united as indissolubly as matter and form. Vergil's epic, the *Aeneid,* is Roman language clothing Greek imagination, and Greek form transfiguring the Roman sense of mission and adventure and responsibility and tradition. (And Dante's *Comedy* and Milton's *Paradise Lost* are both younger, Christian companions and pupils of Vergil's *Aeneid*.)

Peaceful, efficient, productive, law-abiding, intelligent, tasteful, literate, and except in bad reigns and dangerous crises filled with spiritual and personal liberties, that civilization was in most ways the greatest success in social living that our Western world has seen. Far more people could read and write in A.D. 150 than in 1350, or in 1550, or perhaps in 1750 and 1850. The slaves of 200 were better off than the serfs of 1100 or the slaves of 1850, and infinitely better off than the slave-prisoners of German camps in 1944 or Russian camps in 1954. The civilization of Greece and Rome had its imperfections, as all human creations have, but it had more merits to outweigh them than most other cultures in our history. And particularly in the matter of knowledge and of the free dissemination of thought. Schools were nearly everywhere. Europe and northern Africa and Egypt and the Near East were filled with books and covered with libraries. Over thousands of square miles, from city to city, moved the travelling teachers, the wandering philosophers and orators, the religious and social propagandists, freely explaining and eloquently disputing. The best-known document which displays this activity is the Acts of the Apostles. Observe, for example, the sweet reasonableness with which the mayor of Ephesus calms the riot started by St. Paul preaching against idolatry; see how eagerly the Athenian intelligentsia invite him to explain his 'new doctrine' and how civilly they dismiss him when he expounds the resurrection of the body; how calmly the story ends, with St. Paul living in Rome, 'preaching and teaching with all confidence, no man forbidding him'. There were constant disputes in the Greek and Roman world, but they were a sign of the free movement of thought. There was no index of forbidden books. Censorship was sporadic, limited, and trivial. Secret police did not exist as an institution. People conformed far less than they do in any modern national state: in fact, if we could return for a day to Rome or Athens or Marseilles or Antioch as they were in antiquity, we should find them bewilderingly various and eccentric, filled with temptations to moral and intellectual libertinism such as most modern people never encounter. The early Christians suffered far less from the restrictions of the Greco-Roman world than from its liberties. What they wanted was not more freedom, but less.

COLLAPSE, SURVIVAL, REVIVAL

Why that splendid and happy and thoughtful civilization collapsed, no one knows. Its inhabitants themselves did not know. Only the greatest scholars today can assess and group the leading causes. Still, we can be sure of one thing. It was the western part of the empire, the Roman part, that collapsed first; the eastern sector, the Greek-speaking area, maintained itself under almost incessant attacks for another thousand years. And if one were asked to venture a single explanation of that odd disparity, one would do well to say that it came because the men of the West liked wealth and enjoyment, while the men of the East liked thinking. Power and pleasure finally softened the hard Romans and the people of their satellite provinces. The supple Greeks went on talking and arguing and fighting and inventing. If the mind is kept in use, its powers are inexhaustible.

Yet, even after the destruction of the western empire, after the roads had been blocked, the bridges destroyed, the harbours silted up, the aqueducts cut, the drains choked, the hospitals and libraries burnt, the vast public buildings changed into homes for squatters, after language had dissolved into a score of dialects and literacy had become so rare as to be close to magic, when many a priest could scarcely read and many a general or monarch could hardly write his own barbarous name, after the reign of worldwide law had crumbled into the organized gangsterism of the feudal system, even then and thereafter the movement of European civilization is best understood as a process of *learning*. The worst does not last. It did not last even in the Dark Ages. Even while the cities were full of looters wrecking what they could not understand, a few wise optimists were withdrawing into quiet lonely places, and beginning to teach and to copy and to preserve. In a monastery here and a solitary cell there, sat patient students trying to understand the mighty thoughts of the past in prose and poetry, teaching others to understand and transmit them, and so, slowly and gradually, reconstructing the shattered world of the intellect.

Even after attacking and destroying so much of the civilization of the Greco-Roman world, the barbarians learnt from it. Up out of that darkness our ancestors climbed slowly, as their ancestors had climbed before out of far greater darkness, and as our descendants may have to climb once more. It is a long and complex story, for it covers over a thousand difficult years. But if we put the nadir in the West at A.D. 500, we can see three powerful stages in the ascent thereafter: 800, when Charlemagne re-established a supranational political system and reinstituted higher education on a large scale (the type in which this page is printed, the actual forms of the letters, were invented by and for

Charlemagne's scholars); 1150, when the far wider and more intense culture of the Middle Ages was flowering in books and colleges and cathedrals and great minds; and then 1450, when western Europe began more fully to re-possess the full thought of the Greek and Roman world, and to reach out in many ways beyond it. Throughout those thousand years, our predecessors were going to school, first to the Romans and then to the Greeks. By learning, they were civilizing themselves. Since 1450 most of the finest minds in our own civilization have been directly or in-directly the pupils of the Romans and the Greeks; we have not yet learnt all we have to learn from them; there are still barbarians around and among us. Adolf Hitler, with his swastika, his blood rituals, and his hatred of logic, was one of them. There will be others.

Still, it is heartening to gaze back over that long and often interrupted learning process and to see how it brings out so much of the best. We can, for instance, watch the growth of European and American philosophical and re-ligious thought, and see it as a long struggle in which forty generations of thinkers strove to understand and to resist the powerful mind of Plato. We can easily conceive a history of Western oratory, from quiet churches to revolutionary platforms, in terms of the fertilizing genius of Cicero. We can read much of the finest in Western poetry if we merely survey the pupils of Vergil. Or we can record and admire the development of the mind of a single man—Jefferson or Goethe—through his lifelong association with his favourite classical books. St. Paul's and St. Peter's, the Louvre in Paris and the Capitol in Washington, are Greco-Roman build-ings, and much of the thought and art that live within them is the ageless creation of the classical world. Many of the best things in modern Western culture were created or inspired by the Greeks and Romans. If our own civilization should collapse around us, as theirs did, our successors will have to rebuild, like survivors in a bombed city, by using the firm foundations of antiquity and the strongest fragments of what we ourselves shall leave.

IDEAS AND HISTORY

But all this is the story of only one culture. The Greeks taught the Romans. The Romans added much of their own. The modern West civilized itself largely by learning from its parent, the Greco-Roman world. And in our own time perhaps a similar relationship can be divined. In some ways modern Europe—ingenious, argumentative, excitable, both crushed and sustained by its old and opulent tradition of art and thought—is like ancient Greece; and modern North and South America are, in relation to it, like ancient Rome, simpler, cruder, more violent and more practical, bolder and more optimistic, full of respect for the more ancient tradition, but wisely determined to add powers and virtues of their own.

Other civilizations—Chinese, Islamic, Hindu, Amerindian —have quite as wonderful stories of internal development, achieved by the process of patient invention, teaching, and learning within one nation or group of nations. And even more wonderful are the processes by which ideas, techniques, religious beliefs, social and artistic patterns, creations as insignificant as a folk tune and as important as a new science, have passed from one culture to another far removed from it in time, place, and structure, often becoming far more important in the host culture than in their first

3

home, and introducing radical changes in the entire framework of the new civilization they have entered.

Just as the story of any one civilization can and should be told in terms of thinking, learning and teaching (quite as much as through the records of its power and its wealth), so the record of the entire human race, in all its different cultures, can be seen in a new and brilliantly revealing light when we look at the movement of ideas from group to group all over the planet Earth. Many far-reaching changes in history are misunderstood when interpreted in purely political or strategic or economic terms. When studied as intellectual events, they take on their fullest meaning. One brief example from contemporary Asia. There are about ten million Moslems in the Russian empire, mainly Turkish by descent. What is the difference between their subjection to the Tsars and their subjection to the Communists? The difference can be best understood through one fact, and that fact is an educational one. Until after the revolution, all Moslems in the Russian empire used the Arabic alphabet. In the late 1920s it was officially abolished and replaced by a number of alphabets using Roman script (like our own). This was a 'tactical blunder' because the government of Turkey also had determined to use Roman script. Therefore, about 1939, the Latin alphabets also were forbidden. Alphabets based on the Cyrillic script (adapted from Greek and used by the Russians centring on Moscow) were introduced. These two changes show that the intention of the Communist government is to sever the links between these people and their Islamic past and to cut them off from their racial kinsmen in Turkey, transforming them into dependents of Moscow. The Tsars left them alone. The Communists are trying to make them not only Communists but Muscovite

Russians. If they succeed, they will have done so through a compulsory process of teaching and learning.

In fact, the history of much of the twentieth century, with its struggles against communism and fascism and national socialism and so on, will be best written as the record of a war for the command of men's minds. Communism and fascism and national socialism and other forms of state-worship are attractive ideologies, attractive to simple minds. They are collections of ideas partly true and partly false, but imposing in their boldness and clarity, and claiming to give a complete intellectual explanation of the problems of human life. Much of the future of mankind will depend on the skill with which these ideas are taught and rebutted, manipulated to fit different societies and intransigent facts, exploded by penetrating criticisms, or superseded by truer and more effective explanations of the essential problems of existence.

CHAPTER FOUR

The Unpredictable Intellect

YET we cannot foresee the stages of this war in which we are all engaged—the war for the enslavement or liberation of the mind of humanity. The movement of the human intellect is impossible to prophesy: difficult even to record and analyse. Whether we shall ever be able to write a systematic history of thought, explaining the laws that govern its growth and movement, I know not; but at present those who have studied the migration of ideas find it far beyond their powers. Historians such as Sorokin and Toynbee and anthropologists such as Kroeber and Linton have found it hard enough to describe the manifold, the illimitably various stimuli that awaken the sleeping reason and the multiple channels through which thought flows from one mind to another, from one region to another. So far, scholars have been able to establish only the broadest and vaguest rules to assist us in understanding these processes. They are wonders. They are mysteries.

It is difficult, for instance, to see why a single nation should be able in one century to produce a thousand inventors, philosophers, poets, and statesmen, and then, within a few generations, become speechless and apparently thoughtless. Why should one country seethe with intellectual energy as long as it is poor and danger-ridden, only to fall into indolent stupor when it gets wealth and security, while its neighbour, long silent during centuries of poverty and humiliation, finds its voice only after acquiring power and riches? How is it that, within the same country at different times, scientists are now admired and now neglected, poets are sometimes blessed as benefactors and sometimes despised as eccentrics? We know well how often two men, or two groups in different parts of the world, will make the same discovery or think similar thoughts without knowing each other; and that is strange; but it is stranger still to roam through the history of genius, and watch, and see how often mighty minds have appeared in lonely lands and savage tribes and eras full of repression and of hateful violence.

LONELY GENIUS

Sometimes, climbing among the western mountains, one crosses a long wind-lashed and snow-beaten shoulder of harsh broken rocks; and in a tiny hollow halfway across it, see, there is a tuft of bright flowers. Sometimes, from higher up, one looks down into a barren canyon, whose stony walls echo with the dull roar of the torrent below and with the crash of crumbling slabs and pinnacles above: there is not a patch of green, not a visible handful of nourishing earth; but halfway down those precipitous walls, raising its gallant head and spreading its hopeful arms, there grows a pine tree rooted in an invisible notch, and the birds flicker around it.

No less delightful and wonderful is it to read the history of some bloody epoch, crusted with murder and torture, resounding with dull groans, choked hymns, and shouts of senseless violence, and in the midst of it to meet a serene and gracious mind, studying nature and making poetry; or to discover, among lazy bourgeois or glum earthbound peasants, a powerful intellect grappling with abstractions of number, producing unique inventions, or building a systematic interpretation of the universe.

Such was the Buddha. Such was Sequoyah, the Cherokee Indian who, alone, created a written language for his people. Such was the greatest philosopher of the Dark Ages, Johannes Scotus Eriugena—John the Celt from Ireland, as he emphatically called himself—who, almost alone in western Europe at that time, contrived to learn Greek, and created a vast philosophical vision of the spiritual world such as no thinker today could equal. Such was Gregor Mendel, the quiet monk who worked and thought patiently in his garden until he had discovered some of the fundamental laws of heredity. And such were many artists who lived obscurely and whose personalities are all but forgotten, but who made masterpieces of beauty. We may know the name of Aleijadinho, that pathetic figure who became the finest sculptor of Latin America; but the carvers of Chartres are known only by their work, and we cannot even guess the race of the artist who made the exquisite bronze heads from Benin in west Africa.

NEW SYNTHESES

Yet even apart from such lonely geniuses there are other surprises in the history of thought, phenomena almost as unexpected and almost as inexplicable. There are men who express the age and the milieu in which they were educated, but who, by the intensity of their imagination, the sweep of their knowledge, and their astounding versatility, rise high above their era and their neighbours, so that they inhabit both time and eternity at once. When we analyse their minds we can identify nearly all the component elements, tracing this to family and that to school and the other to social climate, and yet the compound is far more than the sum of all these elements: richer, intenser, different in quality as a diamond is different from carbon. Shallow thinkers often fail to understand that this qualitative difference occurs again and again in the realm of the intellect. That is what leads some critics to deny that Shakespeare could have written those plays because he was only a middle-class provincial youth who went from a small-town school to become an actor; and they expect the real author to be someone calculable, like the university-trained lawyer and statesman Bacon, or a witty and graceful young nobleman with the learning and worldly experience of the Renaissance in his very blood. But they are wrong. They are making the elementary error of believing that, in the world of the mind, two and two make four.

Such people can never have taught. One of the few but great rewards of teaching is to see, not once but again and again, how one boy indistinguishable from the others in an average group, will, stimulated by a single remark of the teacher or excited by exploring a new subject, suddenly begin to change. He grows in wisdom; he throws out original ideas of his own; his very speech and handwriting become more mature; he lives on a new time-scale; he changes so rapidly that he distances all his friends and cannot remember or recognize his twelve-months-younger self. Somehow, some happy chance or providential effort has— what can we say? there are no images to describe the event, which is as mysterious as all vital processes—something has caused the energies of his mind, hitherto dissonant or unused, and the emotions with which he once played, or which played with him, to combine into a new, living, active, creative synthesis. This boy astonishes his friends and his parents; usually not himself, for he feels he is simply learning to use powers which are already his own; and never the teacher, who knows the almost limitless treasure of ability and creativity that every pupil carries about in the locked safe of his mind, and who always hopes and strives to unlock it.

And further, those who believe that forces and results in the field of the intellect are always calculable—those who think Bacon or Oxford ought to have written the Shakespearean dramas because that would be easier to understand —must know very little of the personal history of genius. In a touchingly awkward poem representing the shy, self-encouragement of a lonely young man in a far country, John Masefield writes

I have seen flowers come in stony places;
And kindness done by men with ugly faces;
And the gold cup won by the worst horse at the races;
    So I trust, too.

And one certain truth about the great works of the mind—inventions, philosophical systems, poems and plays, pictures and music, scientific discoveries and political institutions—is that many of them were made by men who started life in ordinary, even in unfavourable, situations and then far outsoared their origins.

Isaac Newton was the son of a Lincolnshire farmer: unlike some mathematicians, he was not even bright in boyhood; he was a mediocre student when he went to Cambridge; and then within a few years, the spark descended. Gauss, one of the supreme geniuses of mathematics and electromagnetism, was a village boy like a million others. The founder of modern art-history, Winckelmann, was miserably poor and started as a hack schoolmaster, taking classes all day, sleeping in his schoolhouse, staying awake half the night to teach himself Latin and Greek in preparation for the magnificent career he could only dimly foresee. The by-blow of an Italian gentleman and a country girl was apprenticed to the trade of painting, like many thousands before and after him: but this one was Leonardo da Vinci. Such handicaps hamper but do not crush the growth of the mind: they may even stimulate it. Even the general enemy, ordinariness and routine, cannot always spoil the seed. Loyola, founder of the Jesuits, was a brave ignorant soldier in an age full of stupid men with swords. Luther and Rabelais were monks indistinguishable from myriads of other monks in other lands and times. Socrates was a stonemason in a city crowded with builders. No, the whole history of human thought is as various, as marvellous, as unexpected, and as inexplicable as other mysteries of this universe. Science, with its search for laws, always oversimplifies. But the wise scientist always makes his way through the realm of law into the region of wonder. In a few years he can master the principles of plant and animal life, reproduction, and distribution—and then, for ever thereafter, he remains astounded by the incalculable multiplicity of animal forms, the unthinkable subtlety of plants, knowing that when new varieties are discovered they may contain something as unpredictable as a new divine creation. The complexities of human language, the intricate life of micro-organisms, the invisible radiations that fill the universe, the power of mutation in living forms—all these can be faintly or crudely grasped, but never fully understood. One of the truest sayings of the medieval thinkers was OMNIA EXEVNT IN MYSTERIVM, *All things pass into mystery.* We are not intended only to diagnose and calculate, but also to wonder; to admire; to expect the unexpected.

THE MIND A MYSTERY

Yes, the outer world—both visible and invisible—is ultimately a mystery. So too is the other world we inhabit—the inner world, the world of the mind. Not one of us knows what his own mind contains. Not one of us knows what his own mind can do, or will produce.

Some of the busy and complex activity of the mind is permanently hidden. We can scarcely ever see its vaguest outlines, except now and then in dreams or apparently purposeless actions. Priests at confession, psychoanalysts, listening and probing, lawyers and judges analysing acts of cunning and violence, ethnologists examining myths, and critics penetrating poems, yes, all of us when we listen to music, that wordless language of the soul, experience something of that powerful and terrible world, but can never know it fully. It means to hide itself. The pupils of Freud have sometimes made the problem too simple, saying that the inner activity of the mind was a ferment of 'immoral' or rejected, censored, and repressed material—a living skeleton chained in our cupboard. But the true picture is far more complex. Much of our hidden life literally cannot be dominated, directly helped or impeded, or even understood by our reasoning mind. The instincts, memory, invention, imagination—these and other activities lie largely outside the range of consciousness. The reason can observe them at work, occasionally intervene, and with constant and difficult effort learn to influence them; but their origins, their full power, their methods, all remain beyond its scope. Jesus once asked 'Which of you, by thinking about it, can add a foot to his height?' But we might also ask ourselves whether any of us can forecast what ideas will be put up by his mind a year from now; a week from now; tomorrow; within the next hour.

We are all cave men. The cave we inhabit is our own mind; and consciousness is like a tiny torch, flickering and flaring, which can at best show us only a few outlines of the cave wall that stands nearest, or reflect a dangerous underground river flowing noiselessly at our feet, so that we start back in horror before we are engulfed; as we explore, we come often on shapes of beauty, glittering stalactites, jewel-encrusted pillars, delicate and trusting animals which befriend and follow us; sometimes we even find relics of an earlier time, a primitive statue with flowers still fresh at its feet, or shapes of beasts painted on the wall with bloody handprints beside them; now and then we stumble over a heap that crackles and mutters and moves, but we turn our light away and hurry on; the path we follow sometimes seems to trace an elaborate pattern, although our little flame shows us only a few lines, converging and then curving off into darkness; often its rays die down, threatening to go out altogether and leave us in the resounding gloom; at least thrice in our journey we must crouch down because the cave roof sinks low above us, so that we can go forward only on our knees; when we emerge, it is into another cavern larger than the last but more awesome, where we hear the beat of unseen wings above our head; there are side openings into which our light shines only faintly, to reveal glowing eyes and fearful teeth far in their recesses; the worst of all our trials is that when we venture to speak, the vast invisible walls and roof distort our words into formidable echoes, dying away in superhuman whispers or hateful growls; and, after many a year of wandering, when our torch gleams upon a silent pool and we bend over its calm surface, we do not recognize the face that stares up into our anxious and astonished eyes.

The self is hidden. We do not know ourselves, our brothers and sisters, husbands or wives or children. No friend knows his friend.

Yet all this mystery holds greatness as well as darkness. The cavern is dim, sombre, unexplored; but it contains treasures. Every human brain is filled with unused power. Out of all the billions of men and women who have lived, only a few hundred thousand have been able to employ so much of that power as to change the world. The rest have been dutiful or lazy, good or bad, sensuous or self-denying, thrifty or wasteful, cowardly or brave. Those few hundred thousand, perhaps only a score of thousands in all, are the minds that have made our world. Scientists, strategists, industrialists, aesthetes, explorers, inventors, organizers, authors, musicians, philosophers, doctors and teachers, lawyers and statesmen, several thousands in each class, these are the minds who have given the rest of mankind incalculable benefits, or done it immeasurable damage. They are responsible for much of human history.

Consider the world, apart from mankind. It is either static, or else changing in a gradual and apparently automatic rhythm. The planet swings around the sun, steadily slowing down. The tides flow back and forward with the retreating and returning moon. Weather wears the rocks, the sea eats at the shores, the polar ice advances and recedes. The air and land and water are filled with living things— but they scarcely ever change, or if they do, it is over vast spaces of time. Ferns grow and fish swim and micro-organisms vibrate in our world just as they did long before men walked upon the earth; the industrious ants continue with their routine of self-preservation and self-perpetuation as they did when the dinosaurs ruled. But man, in his brief history, has transformed both the world and himself. His specific quality is purposeful change through thought. He is most truly alive when he thinks.

There are only three secular explanations of history. One is that it is made by groups of people acting together. The second is that historical change is produced by blind impersonal 'forces'. The third is that it is decided and led by powerful individuals. Of course all these theories are true to some extent; and none is true exclusively. Climatic shifts and epidemic diseases move or destroy populations. Social, economic, religious, aesthetic patterns are worked out by successive generations; vast migrations occur without a single leader. Heroes and villains and geniuses preach, rebel, invent, govern. Yet in man's more recent history many of the most powerful and vital changes have been initiated by strong individuals. Not all of these were thinkers. Some were driven by passions of love or hatred or violence or pride. But the work of the thinking man has been more lasting.

Since it is all a mystery, we can never tell how great thinkers emerge. There are very few rules for producing them. They do not grow like trees; they cannot be bred like selected animals. People are not born thoughtless or thoughtful. They become thoughtless or thoughtful. Probably the surest way to grow up stupid is to be part of a large static population doing manual labour and living just on the level of subsistence; and the next best is to be born in a nice family with inherited wealth, brought up in an assured social position, and sent to a quiet and correct school. The young ploughboy and the young marquis are both in a mental prison, one following the furrow, the other set in his comfortable rut.

TRAINING THE THINKER

No, we can never tell how great minds arise, and it is very hard to tell how to detect and encourage them when they do appear. But we do know two methods of feeding them as they grow.

One is to give them constant challenge and stimulus. Put problems before them. Make things difficult for them. They need to think. Produce things for them to think about and question their thinking at every stage. They are inventive and original. Propose experiments to them. Tell them to discover what is hidden.

The second method is to bring them into contact with other eminent minds. It is not enough, not nearly enough, for a clever boy or girl to meet his fellows and his teachers and his parents. He (or she) must meet men and women of real and undeniable distinction. That is, he must meet the immortals. That brilliant and pessimistic scoundrel Plato died just over 2,300 years ago, but through his books he is still talking and thinking and leading others to think; and there is no better way, none, for a young man to start thinking about any kind of philosophical problem—human conduct, political action, logical analysis, metaphysics, aesthetics—than by reading Plato and trying to answer his arguments, detect his sophisms, resist his skilful persuasions, and become both his pupil and his critic. No one can learn to write music better than by studying *The Well-tempered Clavier* of Bach and the symphonies of Beethoven. A young composer who does so will not, if he is any good, write music like Bach and Beethoven. He will write music more like the music that he wanted to write. A man may become a routine diplomat by following the rule book and solving every problem as it comes up, but if he is to grow into a statesman he must read his Machiavelli and consider the lives of Bismarck and Lincoln and Disraeli. The best way toward greatness is to mix with the great.

Challenge and experiment; association with immortal minds: these are the two sure ways of rearing intelligent men and women. And these two opportunities for greatness are, or ought to be, provided by schools and colleges and universities. 'But,' you will ask, 'do schools exist only to train geniuses?' No, but they do not exist only to train the average and to neglect or benumb the talented. They exist to make the best of both. One of the heaviest responsibilities in education is to do justice to exceptional minds, remembering that they may emerge in any place, at any time, and in any body—even a clumsy and misshapen frame may hold a brilliant mind. It must be a strange experience to teach in a little country school, the same subjects year after year to the same families, and then to find a gifted young engineer or a born dramatist among one's pupils. Disconcerting. Difficult. Difficult to know how to encourage without patronizing; difficult not to be a little jealous. Yet the history of knowledge is filled with true stories of teachers who recognized outstanding gifts in a pupil and gave him all he needed to set him on his way to eminence: touching and encouraging, these tales. Such is the story of the Spanish peasant boy who was drawing with charcoal on a plank when a teacher saw him, started training him, and helped to make the artist Goya. Such is the tale of the thin sensitive undersized London schoolboy whose schoolmaster's son gave him the run of his private library: it was among those shelves and as a result of that kindness that the youngster wrote a poem called *On First Looking into Chapman's Homer*. Behind almost every great man there stands either a good parent or a good teacher.

Education in America and in the other countries of the West is an inspiring achievement: all those light, healthy schools, those myriad colleges, so many youngsters having a fine time and not working too hard. Yet it has a couple of weaknesses. One is that education has become almost too easy to get. It is accepted like a supply of pure water: no one expects to get much stimulus or nourishment from it, but it is used to keep the tissues well filled and the outer surface clean. The other is that it does not often carry over into mature life. The average American would rather be driving a car along a crowded highway than reading a book and thinking. The average Frenchman would rather be drinking an extra bottle of wine than watching a play by Racine. The average Britisher would rather fill up a foot-ball-pool form than listen to Elgar's *Enigma*. Why this should be so, I cannot tell. It must be something wrong with education. Probably it is the cult of the average: the idea that schools exist in order to make everyone pretty much the same, and that happiness consists in sharing a group life, sweet, humming, undifferentiated, and crowded like bees in a hive.

Schools do exist for the average. They also exist to serve the distinguished. America was built both by a multitude of common men and women and also by a few eccentrics, heroes, and giants, those whom Stephen Spender exalts when he writes

> I think continually of those who were truly great.
> Who, from the womb, remembered the soul's history
> Through corridors of light where the hours are suns
> Endless and singing.   Whose lovely ambition
> Was that their lips, still touched with fire,
> Should tell of the spirit clothed from head to foot in song
>
> .   .   .   .
>
> Born of the sun they travelled a short while towards the sun
> And left the vivid air signed with their honour.

The life of every teacher is partly dedicated to discovering and encouraging those few powerful minds who will in-fluence our future, and the secret of education is never to forget the possibility of greatness.

We owe them reverence, the great minds of the past and

present and future. It is inspiring and delightful even to scan their names. One shines on another, receiving light in return. It is like looking at the stars, when the eye travels from the Bear to Orion, from Aldebaran to Sirius and Vega, from glory to glory.

When we think of the most majestic mind of the Middle Ages, of Dante, our thought soon travels to his master and companion Vergil, who guided him through Hell and Purgatory until he attained the vision of the beloved; from Dante to the prose counterpart of his poem, the *Summa* of St. Thomas Aquinas; and back from St. Thomas to his master Aristotle. If we read an essay by Francis Bacon, we soon remember the earlier, kinder essayist Montaigne; and then, recalling that Bacon was a scientific thinker, we turn to Descartes, and from him to a kindred mind, Leibniz, and so from greatness to greatness. Descartes and Newton, both interpreted the universe: from Newton it is inevitable to travel back to Kepler and Brahe, forward to Laplace. Sometimes, again, great minds recall each other because, although they were strangers and worked in different media, they saw similar aspects of the universe. It is difficult to play certain fugues by Bach (such as the E flat minor in Book II, full of cold harmonies, meditative rhythms, and sombre melancholy) without thinking of the wise old men with unsmiling wrinkled faces and deep eyes, who watch us from the shadows of Rembrandt's last pictures. It is difficult to look at Dürer's mystical etchings without thinking of Goethe's *Faust*.

Such men were not—as shallow historians try to tell us—creatures of their time and place. Often they were eccentrics who ignored or preceded their epoch; nearly always they were largely self-made; by giving their age a voice and

4

by teaching it, they helped to form it, to dominate it. To read the life of even one such thinker is to renew one's faith in humanity, one's sense of duty to the world. To move freely among the captain minds of any one great age—say the seventeenth century, or the century that produced Cicero, Lucretius, Vergil, Horace, and Livy, or the nineteenth century—is to be perpetually astounded at the depth unplumbable, the infinite variety of the human mind, and to repeat the words of the Greek tragedian:

> Wonders are many, but none,
> none is more wondrous than man.

CHAPTER FIVE

The Future of Knowledge

THE powers of knowledge are unique: incomparable. What is its future? Where will it lead mankind?

Knowledge has not one, but three, possible destinies.

EXPANSION

The first of these is what many of us (not all, but many) hope for. Knowledge may expand and extend, and the work and the abilities of the mind may increase. The most hopeful sign that such a future is being built is the growth of literacy in the world. One could compose a good sound history of civilization in terms of reading, writing, publishing, and book distribution. In the last four or five generations particularly, the advance of literacy has been so rapid and widespread that few of us can fully comprehend it. It is a triumph of the spirit. My father, himself a bookish man, remembered old Scottish weavers who had scarcely had any schooling, and who had taught themselves to read by spelling out a book placed beside the loom while they worked; and I have taught classical Greek to students whose grandparents had spoken no recognized language, only an obscure European dialect which they could not read and in which no books were ever written. That kind of transformation has happened in many parts of the West during the last century, the century of public schools and public libraries. And now we are seeing its extension to other parts of the world. Most of mankind is still illiterate, but now recognizes the importance of books.

Three areas of human effort in which we can hope for massive progress during the next century, and in which progress will most surely benefit humanity, are literacy, land use, and public health. Of these, the one in which most progress is possible is surely literacy.

Together with that, we may hope for the steady expansion of libraries throughout the world. No library is useless. The smallest local collection of books may contain unique treasures or inspire a genius. Every library is an assertion of man's durable trust in intelligence as a protection against irrationalism, force, time, and death. A town or church or school without an adequate collection of books is only half alive. Indeed, libraries are far more necessary now than benefactors like Carnegie ever imagined, because, in the constantly growing flood of useless and distracting appeals to our surface attention—rapidly written magazine articles, flimsy and fragmentary newspapers, and torrents of talk, talk, talk pouring from the radio—they provide a place to rest, be quiet, step off the moving platform of the Moment, and think.

Then applied science and industrial technology, which have so hugely increased our efficiency and comfort in the last century, will surely continue to assist our intelligence by producing new mechanical aids. Although it sounds like a paradox, a great deal of the work of thinkers has always been donkey-work. In 1554 or 1754 it was many times more difficult to become a scholar than in 1954, because one had to expend so much time on preliminaries and details: assembling one's own reference library, transcribing everything by hand, making indexes, searching for unclassified facts, constructing one's own instruments, and relying far too heavily on memory. Even the lighting by which our predecessors read was inferior. But now every branch of knowledge and the work of scholarship and research in general have their own reference libraries, clearly printed, manageable, handsomely indexed; the typewriter and the microfilm are blessings to every student, and further auxiliaries are steadily being developed. About ten years ago Vannevar Bush wrote a remarkable article in which he described the student of some future generation, working at his desk—but a desk that contained a complete library. Set into its top surface were panels of translucent material lit from below, on which the enlargement of a microfilmed page could be thrown (a brighter and clearer thing than the printed page itself); storage space within the desk held thousands of books, records and documents photographed on microfilm rolls, every one indexed and accessible at a single tap of a key; and a transparent platen stood always ready to photograph further material with the turning of a switch. Such equipment is still beyond the reach of most scholars, since they are poor men; yet it is nearer to us than the printed book was to the medieval manuscript. Meanwhile, the experts in electronics are making even more startling aids to research, such as the calculating machine as large as a room, which will do the computation of several hundred mathematicians, or the remembering machine as large as a television set, which will scan, file, and on call repeat every word in a hundred-volume library. The finest of all these mechanisms is one which can store uncountable millions of facts throughout seventy years, and which controls two cameras, two sound recorders, and ten agile and adaptable tools. It is the human brain. But then we have been working on it for hundreds of thousands of years. Its newer extensions will make its operations easier.

We may look forward also to a world-wide organization of scholarship. The history of astronomy alone will show what remarkable progress can be made when learned men in all countries agree to exchange information and to approach large problems in true co-operation. But in most fields of learning, regional and national associations—founded so that their members can share their discoveries and inform and encourage one another—are only three or four generations old. Yet their achievements have been remarkable. The work of the American Association for the Advancement of Science, the British Medical Association, the Association Guillaume Budé, and many others has outrun anything their founders hoped for. There are many discouragements in the work of scholarship. It is badly paid; much of it is done in isolation, and after repeated failures a lonely man becomes pessimistic; even teaching is not much of a stimulus sometimes, because students have to be shown the elements of a subject while advanced research is beyond their understanding; the rest of the world seems to admire and to reward the charlatans and confidence tricksters: what wonder if the scholar sometimes slows down, or thinks of abandoning his work? But at the regular meetings of a group that shares his interests he can reassure himself that his work is important, recall the distinguished men of the past, and meet the young men who are to advance his subject in the future. Now, a visit to an international meeting of scholars is even more stimulating. It rises above personal competition and local rivalry. True, it often exacerbates national passions; but wise leadership and the growth of custom will help to overcome them. A thinker who has never troubled to define his principles because he has been teaching within the narrow frontiers of his own country, or a group of scholars which has been working half-instinctively in co-operation, will at such a congress take pains to formulate aims and methods so that all (including themselves) can understand them clearly. By observing demonstrations of new techniques suggested by local or national experience, by criticizing enthusiasms or questioning assumptions expressed in discussion, and later by reviewing different approaches to a single theme, every scholar loses his feeling of lonely inadequacy, and becomes convinced that—as well as being Dr. A of B-ville in C-land—he is an organ of the activity which is both human and superhuman, the reason of mankind.

Until recent years, international scholarly meetings have been occasional, and most of their sponsoring bodies have been impermanent. Some world societies for intellectual co-operation were growing up in that splendid period of happiness and promise, the early years of the twentieth century, but the First World War disrupted them. The effect of the Second, however, was to encourage them again. Since 1945 there have been many valuable international congresses, and more are now being arranged every year: festivals of music, of the film, conventions of historians, of food experts, of papyrologists, of foresters. One of the chief aims of the United Nations Educational, Scientific and Cultural Organization (UNESCO) is to stimulate and regularize such meetings. UNESCO is a new cell of the world brain.

So far most research is published in national periodicals— *Klio, Chemical Engineering Progress, La Revista de Filologia Española, Die Zeitschrift für analytische Chemie, The Lancet,* and so forth—and a fatiguing part of every scholar's duty is to find and read the articles of his colleagues, printed in a dozen different languages. There are a few international digests of learning, and a few international periodicals like *Erasmus* (published in Switzerland and edited by a board of savants from two continents); but not enough. There is a fine opening here for one of the wealthy foundations to establish a series of quarterly reviews covering all the most important fields of learning, drawing contributions from all over the world, and written in the three or four principal culture-languages; or perhaps to grant UNESCO sufficient capital to start such reviews, in the expectation that library subscriptions would be sufficient to support them thenceforward.

For young students also there are associations which enable them to spend part of their college life, a year or half a year, in a foreign land. This type of enterprise also is being sponsored by UNESCO. Some idealists believe that such exchanges will help to discourage future wars. Anyone who realizes the tremendous power of most national governments and the irrationality of most wars may doubt that they will; but at least they will assist the survivors in picking up the pieces and beginning to re-establish a world unity.

That is the future that many of us hope for: the expansion of knowledge throughout the world. But there are at least two other possibilities.

SELF-DESTRUCTION

One of these possibilities is that the human mind may commit suicide. Most people respect knowledge, but they do not necessarily like it. The pessimist Swift even said that the mass of men was as well qualified for flying as for thinking. Suppose that the standard of living continues to rise all over the world, as it has done in the last century; that the population continues to increase; that its labours are shortened, its hours of leisure lengthened, its anxieties diminished, and its pleasures more lavishly supplied. Which will it prefer, learning or liquor? Art, music, and books, or cards, dice, and horse races?

It is difficult to be sure. All over the planet, as soon as men and women get a little money and leisure, something to lift them above the hunger of this week and the apprehensions of next year, at once their diversions tend to become either silly or disgusting. Whether you think money represents extra work (the product of so many hours of labour) or material (oil and other minerals drawn out of the earth, plants and animals grown upon it, power produced by using its energies), it is appalling to reflect upon the billions of hours and the masses of material which are utterly wasted every single day all over the world, by being thrown away on trashy amusements, none of them providing more than a single day's excitement, most of them offering much less, and all of them based on the idea of Having a Good Time, which really means having a momentary impulse and satisfying it. We must be related to the monkeys, because so few of us seem to realize that pleasure is not the same as happiness.

Now, it is certainly possible that the future of human thought is this: that it will be swamped under a flood of human silliness. Nations and civilizations which discover how much easier and jollier it is to live for transient pleasures, without troubling about anything permanent in the world of the mind, soon find that their mental muscles turn flabby, that they cannot think about certain difficult problems at all and prefer to substitute bursts of emotional energy for sustained intellectual effort, and eventually that they have barbarized themselves more delightfully but not less completely than through submitting to an invasion of savages. They have become, like many primitive tribes, unable to read and write, incapable of organizing their experience into a logical pattern, impotent to plan for changes in the future or to recall the lessons of the past.

This has already happened in part of our civilization. Although no one knows all the reasons for the collapse of the western Roman empire, and although there must be many different and convergent reasons, one of them was evidently that men and women began to have too good a time, and simply stopped thinking. There are some historical novels which depict the rise of Christianity as a movement of rebellion, the humble and oppressed rising with a pure vehemence of irresistible protest against the intolerable tyranny of helmeted legionaries and cruel tormentors. Nonsense. The early Christians repeat again and again that life around them is *too pleasant*, everyone can have a Good Time, every lust can be satisfied and new lusts are constantly being invented. Wealth and pleasure and thoughtlessness, these made the 'world' which the Christians endeavoured to transmute, or from which they fled in despair. Eventually they converted it, just as it was collapsing, and as we know, they preserved much of the best of it, the books and the ideas of those who had thought and written while the others around them spent life and wealth on girls, drink, and the races.

Therefore this could happen to our civilization again. Some observers believe it is happening now—not over all the Western world, nor over all the planet, but at least in several countries. They are convinced that the pursuit of money and temporary pleasure is killing all other powers of the spirit and corrupting society. Eliot thinks that when we pass away the wind will blow over the ruins of our homes, saying

> Here were decent godless people :
> Their only monument the asphalt road
> And a thousand lost golf balls.

Robinson Jeffers believes that riches and lusts have smothered the heroism, purity of motive, and nobility that created the American republic and for many years sustained it. There are others who think the same of their own countries, in Britain, in Australia, in Brazil, in France. . . .

Worse than that. You remember how, when the Japanese invaded China twenty years ago, they paid special attention to the opium traffic, legalizing and encouraging it throughout the occupied areas, making it as easy as possible for their subjects to become addicts. The Germans did the same with vodka in occupied Poland. During Machado's dictatorship in Cuba, whenever his secret police foresaw an uprising, any expression of protest or cry of independent will, they announced programmes of indecent films in the Havana theatres, to turn men's minds to other things. Drugs are a weapon.

It would be perfectly possible, therefore, to corrupt the majority of a nation, perhaps of a whole region, by feeding them drugs, an incessant supply of petty pleasures intended to degrade their character and dull their minds. It would be possible to demoralize millions of people by making life easy for them, so that they forgot to use their brains. The emperors of Rome scarcely needed a secret police because they supplied the Roman populace with free meals, frequent gifts of money, and in one year as many as 150 days of spectator sports—prize-fighting (with swords, not boxing gloves), super-colossal three-dimensional pageants, and horse-and-chariot races. Could a modern nation resist a lavish programme of 'home relief', free TV sets for everyone, systematized and legalized gambling, cheap liquor, free football, baseball, boxing, wrestling, dirt-track contests, bathing-beauty shows, races, and movies seven days a week? There is a grim political saying that the Many are always the servants of the Few. Usually the Many are held down by feudalism or some other oppressive social and political pattern but sometimes it is possible for clever cynical men to control them by supplying them with drugs, by keeping them from reading good books or thinking original thoughts, changing them ultimately into idiots by giving them a Good Time. Just so, at the sovereign yawn of the goddess of stupidity in Pope's mock epic of self-delighted idiocy,

Art after Art goes out, and all is night.

.   .   .   .   .

Religion, blushing, veils her sacred fires,
And unawares Morality expires.
Nor public flame, nor private, dares to shine;
Nor human spark is left, nor glimpse divine!
Lo! thy dread empire, Chaos! is restored;
Light dies before thy uncreating word:
Thy hand, great Anarch! lets the curtain fall;
And universal darkness buries all.

There, then, is a second possible future of knowledge. It might be smothered, deliberately by a controlling group, or else unwittingly and witlessly by ourselves. Art might degenerate into decoration or amusement. Spiritual efforts might be replaced by 'stimuli'. Thought might be abandoned by the multitude, left to a few 'specialists' and 'experts'. Everyone might have a life of pleasure, and the world would come to look more and more like those odd prehistoric societies which we can divine from their remains. They dwelt along the shores of the sea, picking up shellfish and eating them; shellfish were plentiful, the people had no enemies but winter and rough weather, they lived with full bellies and empty minds year after year, generation unto generation, and all we know of them now is an enormous series of dumps, hundreds of feet thick, made of discarded sea shells and debris. They are called the Kitchen Midden People.

THOUGHT CONTROL

The third possibility is that human thought will be deliberately and forcibly controlled and limited. This also has already happened a number of times in history; it is happening now. The aim of those who try to control thought is always the same, and they always work on the same principle. They find one single explanation of the world, one system of thought and action that will (they believe) cover everything; and then they try to impose that on all thinking people.

Critics discussing the imposition of belief usually write as though every normal man hated it, the currents of thought throughout history set against it, and only a minority of brutal and Machiavellian masters attempted to enforce it. This is wishful imagination rather than cool analysis. However absurd a system of belief may look from outside, or in the perspectives of history, it can often be made acceptable to the average man by several powerful factors of attraction. The most obvious of these attractions is the delightful sense of belonging to a *group*—a group which shares all its beliefs, which is superior to other groups, and which often calls itself 'the Elect', 'the One Party', 'God's People', or even gods incarnate. An equally important attraction is the charisma of a *leader,* the inspiring and controlling influence of a personality which combines kindness and power, persuasion and authority: the Apostle, the Leader, the Mahatma. And, thirdly, such systems rest on a *revelation,* a series of statements or assumptions that cannot be questioned. For example, the Communists believe that historical change in the future is immutably destined to proceed along a pattern invented by Hegel and adapted by Marx. The Mormons believe that Joseph Smith of Palmyra, New York, was visited by an angel who showed him a set of golden tablets explaining that the inhabitants of America before Columbus were descended from the Jews, and that he read the tablets through a pair of golden spectacles which turned their 'reformed Hebrew' writing into English. These beliefs are not to be treated as probable or improbable, possibly verifiable or possibly false: they are to be accepted as true, exactly as it is true that $2 \times 2 = 4$. The average man finds it a comfort to start from such a firm basis. And the fourth and final attraction about these systems is their claim to be *complete*. The single revelation contains everything. The answer to all life's problems is here, incapsulated in this Doctrine, this System—and in no other. Ever since we became human we have been puzzled. Therefore it is a profound happiness to find some teaching which seems to satisfy all our wonder and to answer all the questions we can ask about human existence.

Throughout the world, most people accept one of these closed systems of belief. And when a critic questions it, they hate him: not only because he is a choplogic, but because he is rejecting their revelation, and profaning the charisma of their leader, and attacking the group to which they belong. Usually they do not argue with him. That they leave to the trained expositors. Instead, like the Asiatic Greeks during St. Paul's mission to Ephesus, they assemble together and all with one voice for the space of about two hours cry out 'Great is Diana of the Ephesians!' or else, like the Jews when Paul spoke of preaching to the Gentiles, 'Away with such a fellow from the earth!'

It is easy, therefore, in fact it is often an expression of the will of the majority, to silence all questioning of established systems of belief and to regard critics as heretics, heretics as damned criminals. Throughout much civilized history most people have lived within such systems, approving the condemnation of heretics. Accordingly, it is perfectly possible that, within the next century or so, all human thought will be fitted into one or more new systems, with all the usual accompaniments of quasi-divine authority, group solidarity, and emotional satisfaction. Our present age of adventure, disorder, and revolution may well be followed by an era of rigid orthodoxy. Already we can see thoughtful men in several countries choosing orthodoxy either because they are frightened or because they wish to avoid what they believe is its only alternative, anarchy. *The Captive Mind*, a recent book by a Polish poet who was 'brain washed' by the orthodoxy presently established in his own country, vividly describes the cynicism, despair, and schizophrenic madness that the process created in the inmates of that new prison. But, after a few increasingly docile generations had passed through orthodox schools and colleges, had read and written nothing but orthodox books, had been warned against the disgusting horrors of heterodoxy, and had grown used to the comfortable routine of acceptance, then, for a time at least, even the most intelligent might possibly settle down, like well-conditioned animals in a laboratory, to accept the invisible barriers that represent the glass walls and electric currents from which they once recoiled, to retreat from freedom of thought as from an intolerable, inconceivable exertion, and to enjoy the tame familiar process of solving the problems of their own brave new world, smaller but safer, meaner but tidier, than the vast incomprehensible universe.

CHAPTER SIX

The Voice out of the Whirlwind

THREE friends sit with their friend in silence. A thoughtful and God-fearing man, he was once illustrious and wealthy. But suddenly, like bombs falling out of the darkness, disasters have blown his life into fragments. His children have been massacred, his wealth has vanished. Bereaved and beggared, he is attacked by a hideous disease. He has nothing to look for but death. His disease gives him misery without extinction. His entire life, all he ever did and thought, has become meaningless. Although his friends come to console him, he cannot even see them at first, nor can they speak to him.

After days and nights, he opens his mouth for the first time, to speak. He curses the day on which he was born. He wishes he had never even drawn the first breath of life, since human existence is either meaningless or cruel. A meaningless life is not worth living. A cruel life is a trap set by a divine devil.

His friends are horrified. They came to console him, and to help him in repenting of his sins, but not to hear him denounce the universe. They cannot believe that he is condemning the whole of life, for that would be equivalent to blasphemy; and they cannot agree to call life meaningless.

They tell him that he must have done something wicked. He is a sinner. That is why he is suffering.

No. He denies it. He has led a life as righteous as is possible for a human being. His ruin cannot be a just punishment. No one can be condemned for doing his best. Therefore the cruelty of the world is irrational and God's justice is no justice. His friends reject this with horror. Again and again, over their protests, he calls for a reason. He can see none. They can give him none that he will accept.

After long and powerful assertions and counter-assertions, forming a drastic debate on this agonizing problem, the afflicted man and his friends fall back into silence. Another speaker is heard for a while, babbling, but he is soon stilled. All human speech is useless; all human thought is helpless in such a chaos.

Then over the four men rises the sound that clamoured through the earth before any human being lived to hear it: the sound of a mighty storm. Far more than human speech, this is the voice of the universe. The sufferer hears it. Out of it God speaks to him. Not reassuring words, nor kindly promises, but a long, an overpowering series of unanswerable questions rolling out like repeated peals of thunder divided by sudden blinding visions like lightning flashes, questions that grow into something greater, into a proclamation of power, wonder, and glory. The universe is neither good nor bad, neither just nor unjust—such names are too petty. The universe is a mystery. As a cloud encloses force, the universe contains grandeur. Man must question, for that is his nature. Man must believe that God is righteous, even by asking how. But his chief duty, before questioning and belief, is to feel awe. He is small. God's universe is great. He is limited in time and space. It is endless and infinite. He can

5

know a little and ask more. It is full of things he can never
know, intricacies and magnificences he can neither experience nor comprehend. The distant star and the powerful
bird of prey obey laws he did not make, cannot control, and
can only dimly understand. The voice rises again and again
in thunder-music:

> Canst thou bind the sweet influences of Pleiades,
>   or loose the bands of Orion?
> Canst thou bring forth Mazzaroth in his season?
>   or canst thou guide Arcturus with his sons?
> Doth the hawk fly by thy wisdom,
>   and stretch her wings toward the south?
> Doth the eagle mount up at thy command,
>   and make her nest on high?

As the voice rolls away into the recesses of heaven, the
afflicted man bows his head, not in suffering but in wonder
and humility. The government of the universe must be
beyond human knowledge. Although thought is vital to our
life, it can never reach far enough. Beyond thought, there is
a vision, and the sense of awe.

> I have uttered that I understood not :
>   things too wonderful for me, which I knew not.
> I have heard of thee by the hearing of the ear :
>   but now mine eye seeth thee.

And so, with amazement and with the admission of
human inadequacy, closes one of the greatest works of
Hebrew poetry and religious imagination, the Book of Job.
No one knows who wrote it. Indeed it seems that several
different writers worked on it, and it is clear that its two
main parts were the creation of two geniuses: one who
composed a declaration of the insolubility of suffering,

man's complaint against God; and another who replied by proclaiming, in truly prophetic tones, that the whole universe is beyond human knowledge and yet is worthy of praise and prayer. Something can be understood. Something can be divined. All cannot be known.

CHAPTER SEVEN

All Cannot be Known

THE Book of Job puts into poetry one of the central experiences of every human being. It is an experience which begins early in childhood, which (unless it is benumbed or smothered) lasts into extreme old age, which often drives men further than other passions, and which has produced far more of the achievements that distinguish us from the beasts. It is the sense of wonder.

Strange, that sense. It combines the wish to know with the knowledge that all cannot be known. It is perpetual surprise. It accepts logic and science, then passes beyond them and forgets them. Within every one of us, from the savage in the Amazon jungle to the analyst in the laboratory, from the Swedish factory-girl to the Malayan fisherman, from the diplomat to the detective, from the poet to the ploughman, there is a pleased and competent acceptance of what can be recognized and dealt with—but together with that, there is an astonished awareness of inflowing mystery. Even the most practical and successful of men, triumphant millionaire or powerful statesman, looks back into his own past with amazement at the hazards he escaped and the failures he survived; and knows that he cannot possibly foresee even the events of the next twenty-four hours. The dullest and most hopeless drudge glances up from time to time because something strange occurs, and he continues to live because not all the future can be plotted. The wisest scientist finds that every discovered truth leads into further questions yet unapprehended, and must constantly pause, 'like some watcher of the skies when a new planet swims into his ken', to gaze at the simplest of his subjects, a leaf, a bacillus, a drop of blood, or a rock, as though he had never seen it before in all his life, and knew his mind could never fully grasp it.

Our mind wishes to take in everything, yet knows it cannot. There is the paradox. Knowledge must know its own limits.

Clearly there are two different types of limitation upon human knowledge. One kind is imposed by human beings themselves. The other is inherent in the structure of the mind and its relation to the universe. The friends of Job suffered from the first. Job himself learnt to recognize the second.

CHAPTER EIGHT

External Hindrances

THE human mind is capable of far more work than it has ever done. A normal man uses nearly all his muscles during his mature life, but leaves large areas, perhaps two thirds, of his brain dormant. Not even the greatest creative thinker has ever complained that his intellect was too weak to serve him, that he found it a dull and clumsy tool, but rather that he was approaching death before he learnt all its uses.

Then why are there so many ignorant and stupid people in the world?

Surely it is because some of them, as individuals, misuse their minds, while others live in societies that discourage thought.

SLOTH

Individually, many people throughout the world are simply lazy. The bright adventurous intelligence which they enjoyed in their youth is allowed to lie virtually unused for the rest of their seventy years, covered over with the sediment of routine, rusted by the constant drip of casual gossip, clogged by meaningless chatter from newspaper and radio, employed only on daily problems and the incessant re-examination of personal reminiscences. Often an active mind forces its way out of the cocoon and cries for work, and then its owner gives it false and fruitless work to do. Many a man who unconsciously loathes the boredom of his life will relieve it by thinking—but by thinking about the wrong subjects. He will memorize the first, second, and third horses in all the major races for forty years, or the batting averages of two thousand leading players. Many a woman finds her greatest intellectual pleasure in collecting and arranging an immense volume of gossip and genealogy, who married whom, who is whose cousin, what are the weaknesses of each particular family, that house has never had good luck, all the Svensen girls have a silly streak, they get it from their grandmother, she was a Vestrup, came from Goldfoss in the year the brindle cow died, a very wet autumn, spoilt all my bleaching for three weeks, on and on, enough to fill a whole bookshelf with personal reminiscence. And lastly, many an otherwise intelligent man or woman wastes his or her intellect by failing to train and use it properly, by assembling masses of utterly unco-ordinated facts and unverified information, then building on them. Such people become local eccentrics, hollow-earth fanatics, amateur metaphysicians: they are not fools; but they have minds, and spoil them.

But most of the waste of intellect is caused by society. Looking over all the world, at the two billion minds of which so many are paralysed or crippled, we must feel as sad as a doctor when he sees that the majority of human bodies are badly fed, stupidly treated in their ailments, crippled by silly fashions in clothes and housing, sometimes allowed to degenerate through stupidity and sometimes maimed or deformed through malice. Socially, minds are limited by three agencies: poverty; error; and deliberate purpose.

POVERTY

Of course, poverty is the main limitation. As Johnson, following the Roman Juvenal, wrote,

> Slow rises worth, by poverty depress'd.

Most of the human race live just above the bare level of subsistence: they can scarcely afford to buy books or to pay teachers or to build schools. Colleges, laboratories, libraries, universities, are beyond them utterly. After every major war, this is one of the principal dangers to the mind. Books and schools have been destroyed: it is hard to replace them rapidly; and the youngsters are growing up half savage. This is why civilization disappears so quickly in a succession of wars. Education depends on tradition, organization, and equipment. Remove these three for only fifty years, and the land is full of illiterates. That is the most appalling thing about the onset of the Dark Ages in Europe fifteen centuries ago. In A.D. 400 books were plentiful, almost oversupplied; and eight or ten generations later a book was a precious thing, guarded, revered, by most people scarcely understood. A scholar would write across war-torn and bandit-ridden wastes asking whether his friend in some distant Shangri-La owned a certain book, and if so whether he would lend it to be copied and returned. St. Columba, the missionary from Christian Ireland to the Scots, quarrelled with St. Finnian about the ownership of a single book which he had written out, night after night, copying St. Finnian's own text: the dispute degenerated into a clan fight after King Diarmait of Ireland decided that the copy belonged to St. Finnian 'as to every cow belongs her calf'. I never look at a volume written in those Dark Ages, with its big cowhide pages and its laborious lettering, but I have a sense of admiration for the scribe who slowly wrote it out and for the librarians who carefully preserved it through centuries of war, looting, and ignorant neglect—and I have renewed hope and confidence in the future of mankind. Should any such catastrophe afflict us too, we shall do our best to help one another. The surviving doctors and nurses will set up some simple plans for public health and medical training. The churchmen will continue their service to God even among the debris. The engineers will improvise communications and transport and services with what tools they can salvage or contrive. And as for the teachers, they will start searching the ruins for books and laboratory equipment, and open a school.

And yet poverty, even the poverty of an entire society, is not an insurmountable barrier to education if people are determined to learn and prepared to sacrifice. An entire society can raise its standards within fifty years by a concerted effort, or maintain them for centuries against persistent discouragement. Finland is one of the poorest nations in Europe, but it has splendid schools, and its citizens are far more cultivated than many a richer nation. Scotland was never wealthy; yet she has supported four universities ever since the Renaissance, and the annals of each of them are filled with tales of peasant boys reared in grinding poverty and scarcely able to buy a suit of clothes, still winning their way to college, living there on a sack of oatmeal and a few salt herrings brought from their cottage homes, and rising to distinction as scholars and inventors. Most astonishing of all, perhaps, is the tenacity with which the Jews, living for many generations in the poor ghettoes of eastern Europe, kept up their own school system, transmitted their books faithfully through the centuries, and added to them a mass of explanation, symbolism, and decoration which is a monument to the power of the human mind as well as an act of homage to God.

ERROR

Poverty is wretched, but error is maddening. It sickens the soul to think how many good minds have been stultified or discouraged or misguided all over the world throughout many centuries of education. Sometimes standards have been set too high, so that the average boy and girl are neglected and many a potential talent is snuffed out. Often and often, a decent education has been offered only to a chosen group, the rest left to consume their souls in ignorance. Only within the lifetime of people now among us have women been generally admitted to share the culture of their nation and the world: and that in a few countries only. Every Brahmin boy in southern India is well schooled, but how hard it has been for a low-caste youngster to learn to use his gifts, even to discover whether he is gifted! Sometimes the structure and history of a society makes education too rare and difficult and specialized. Thus, in China there is no spoken Chinese language, only a number of mutually unintelligible dialects, and a single system of written characters which corresponds to no single dialect and is appallingly difficult to learn. Therefore education in China has necessarily been reserved for a small minority who are good at memorizing visual symbols and at thinking abstractly. And in many societies the external rituals of religion and social life have become immensely complicated, so that much good brain-power is spent on memorizing and elaborating inessential, accidental relationships and sounds. For centuries past, talented youths in many countries have spent years learning by heart intricate scriptures and hymns—often in languages only half understood—so that they can repeat them without misplacing a syllable and yet without analysing or assimilating their full meaning. Most anthropologists are astounded by the intellectual energy which a Tibetan or Navaho youth will put into memorizing every stage of a complex ceremony, in which the cow-tail whisk must have exactly seventeen tassels, and the blue square must be balanced by a crimson circle, and the holy box must contain eighty-five beads, no more and no less; and by the fantastic accuracy with which a fisherman in a tiny river village can define his relationships with the Turtle totem, the Salmon clan, the Fishhawk sept, and the secret societies that criss-cross within those laboriously complex systems. Sometimes it looks as though people deliberately arranged their lives in order not to think about the essentials.

But minds are also wasted through being taught ineffectively, by teachers who have narrow aims, or in schools which are too easy and slack. Our memories are still full of the caricatures drawn by writers of a hundred years ago, showing grim schoolmasters, cane in hand, terrorizing groups of cowering children. All that was part of early-nineteenth-century Puritanism, and (for good or bad) is long since obsolete. A modern satirist would tell more truth if he inverted the caricature, and showed the teacher shrinking before the annual inflow of self-satisfied shallow-minded boors, compelled to coax where he ought to command, and attempting to maintain his own integrity, enthusiasm, love of humanity, and interest in learning, by murmuring 'Forgive them, for they know not what I do'. Universal education is still a novel experiment in our culture; yet its gloomy obverse is already clear to view. All people do not want to be educated. Many resist education all their lives. When education is not a privilege, it easily becomes a burden. Teachers in the new state universities and the compulsory schools sometimes feel like doctors endeavouring to explain to an unwilling patient that pure food is better than tainted food, or to persuade mothers to put their children to sleep with milk rather than gin.

Now, in the Western world, there are three errors which

help to account for the weaknesses of contemporary education.

The first is the mistaken idea that schools exist principally to train boys and girls to be sociable, 'integrated with their group', 'equipped with the skills of social living', 'adjusted to family and community co-operation', and so forth. Obviously that is *one* of the aims of schooling, sometimes neglected in the past though usually emerging as a by-product. It was a necessary and valuable function of school and college at the most recent stage in American history to create a more or less uniform pattern of culture for the new middle class, and a stable social order in which the children of the unparalleled flood of immigrants who reached the country between 1880 and 1920 could find their place as Americans. But another aim of education, equally important or more important, is to train the individual mind as intensely and to encourage it as variously as possible—since much of our better and our more essential life is lived by us as individuals, and since (in the advancing age of mass-culture) it is vital for us to maintain personal independence.

The second of these three errors is the belief that education is a closed-end process, which stops completely as soon as adult life begins. During the war a friend of mine was in a unit (it might have been in any of the Western armies) where no one was illiterate, but no one ever opened a book. He bought paper-backed novels and collections of essays to read in the long hours of boredom which are inseparable from military life. As he turned page after page and went through book after book, the others watched him with bewilderment. Finally, as he threw away the fifteenth volume and opened the sixteenth, one of his buddies came up and said 'Studyin' all the time, don't you never get tired?'

This fellow could not imagine that reading a book could possibly be anything but work—hard, exhausting work. Just in the same way many of the young people who graduate from schools and colleges in Europe, in North and South America, in Australia and elsewhere, immediately drop their languages, forget their science (unless they move into a scientific job), abandon their economic and political thinking, and fail to relate their four or eight years of intellectual training to the rest of their lifetime. It is like learning music for nearly a decade, and then never going to a concert or playing a single note. Here the schools, colleges, and teachers are surely to blame. Too many teachers (especially in college) seem to limit the interest of their students by implying that their own true and central aim is to train professional scholars, and that amateur interest in their subject is to be deprecated.

The third error which limits the use of knowledge in the Western world is the notion that learning and teaching always ought to have immediate results, show a profit, lead to success. Now, it is true that education is intended to benefit the entire personality. But it is not possible, not even desirable, to show that many of the most important subjects which are taught as part of education will make the learner rich, fit him for social life, or find him a job. Some values must be postulated. Poetry is better than pinball. The man who does not know anything about biology is in that respect inferior to the man who does, even although he may be richer in pocket. A training in philosophy makes few men wealthy, but it satisfies an instinct in them which cries for fulfilment as hungrily as the drives to survive and to reproduce, and which is less easily sated. People who know no history always learn wrong history, and can never understand the passing moment as it changes into history. Yet sometimes it is difficult to convince young people of this, difficult even to explain it to parents and to school supervisors. The result is that important and long-fruitful subjects tend to be squeezed out of education, neglected, even ignored and deformed. For instance, English literature is one of the finest literatures in the entire world: a thing to be proud of and to enjoy. To be brought up speaking and reading English is to be presented with the key to a massive and incorruptible treasure. Our literature from Chaucer to Eliot contains enough to make a man happy, thoughtful, and eloquent through an entire lifetime. And yet many unfortunate boys and girls in the English-speaking countries are being denied that opportunity. Their teachers tell their parents that language is a 'tool'; and instead of showing them how to read and appreciate the best fifty of those miraculous books, they instruct them in a dreary pastiche sometimes called 'language arts', which is to literature as finger painting is to the National Gallery. Year by year, more youngsters go to high school and to college. Year by year, standards go down and down—and not because there is an inevitable degradation in admitting large crowds into our educational system, but simply because we are recklessly ready to waste both the minds of the young and the rich inheritance of the past.

RESTRICTIONS

There remains one further type of external limitation on knowledge. This is deliberate restriction, by political or social or ecclesiastical authority. Is such restriction ever justifiable? If so, when and why? How far should it extend, and how should it be limited? These are hard questions. They have been eagerly discussed, because they interest and excite people very keenly. Many books have been written about them: so many that they almost obscure the principles which must underlie any attempt to answer them.

To begin with, it is obvious that there must be some restraints on the right to knowledge. Society is based on the equable limitation of rights, for the benefit of its members.

Individual Privacy. Thus, no one has a right to know, far less to publish, details of the private life of another citizen in so far as they are genuinely private. No one has any right to acquire and to disseminate information about the actions of a fellow citizen unless they clearly affect the interests of some other person or the welfare of the whole community. If I discover that ten years ago my neighbour served a term in prison, during which his wife had a child by another man, I have no right to pass that knowledge to the general public, none whatever, unless it can be shown that the public interest would be injured by concealing it. *The greater the truth* (say the lawyers), *the greater the libel.* There are certain regions of life in which it is essential to protect the individual against other individuals, against groups, and against society. Obviously the most important of these is his right to choose a political representative to support his interests. It is to protect this right that we sacrifice something of the right to knowledge, and lay down that a citizen's vote must be kept secret.

Group Privacy. Similarly, any group has a right to protect itself, provided that it has a legal and moral right to exist. Therefore it can prevent the free use of knowledge which might be prejudicial to it. Every business has its secrets, which it has purchased or discovered. The general

public is not entitled to knowledge of these secrets unless
and until the interest of the entire community demands it.
This is because society exists for the sake of individuals and
groups of individuals; individuals and groups do not exist
for the sake of society. (Of course, there have often been
communities which tried to abolish individual life altogether,
making every act, word, and thought open and communi-
cable; but they have been small, temporary, specialized, or
low in spiritual and intellectual charge.) On a larger scale,
groups organized as churches, parties, or nations do in
practice keep their secrets, and most people would hold that
humanity at large has no right to knowledge of them—
unless and until they threaten the welfare of humanity. The
Roman Catholic Church does not hold that the public has
a right to know the sources and dimensions of its income,
or the exact disposition of its investments. The Swiss are a
peaceful people, and they admire the progress of science;
and yet only a very naive or treasonous Swiss would declare
that the location of every mine and battery in the Swiss
defence system ought to be published, even although thereby
the advance of military science would be assisted. So also
every nation possesses essential secrets which cannot be
disclosed to the whole world without endangering its independent existence, by assisting its actual or potential
enemies. No doubt, if and when international peace is firmly
established, the peoples of the earth and their governments
will have no secrets from one another. But this does not by
any means prove that the publication of national secrets at
this stage of history will assist the establishment of international peace: particularly since most of the wars recently
fought and expected in the foreseeable future have been
encouraged not by ignorance of facts but by emotional

tensions, unreasoned ambitions, long-standing hatreds, and crusading faiths. No amount of documentation will endear the Germans to the Poles or lead the Arabs to trust the Jews: it is a waste of effort to attempt to solve such problems by the dissemination of knowledge.

Censorship. Now, within a single society, are there any necessary limitations of the right to knowledge? From the practice of every human society, it appears that there are. Societies are not harmonious organizations of individuals. Every nation contains anti-social men and women; and many a human being is irresponsible and dangerous, to society and to himself, at certain stages, in his life. In practice, therefore, limitations on knowledge are devised in order to protect society against the anti-social and the irresponsible.

To take the easiest example, would it be wise to publish or broadcast to an entire nation the exact methods of making simple but deadly poisons and cheap but formidable explosives? Obviously not. A diligent researcher in a public library can discover the facts for himself; there is in most countries no express legal prohibition against issuing a handbook containing such facts; but society effectively discourages their publication, contriving to restrict the knowledge of them to those technicians who have a responsible and legitimate purpose for using them. Similarly, there is no legal obstacle in many countries to prevent a publisher from making money by printing a booklet giving the easiest and safest means of inducing abortion; such knowledge does circulate in certain groups; but it is not, and it ought not to be, freely disseminated.

It becomes more difficult when we ask how to control irresponsible people *before* they commit anti-social acts, by limiting their knowledge. During the last few generations this question has been long and loudly discussed in the United States and other countries. It has not been solved. Intelligent men and women hold diametrically opposite views on it. Some are afraid, terribly afraid, of censorship in any form whatever. Others see even greater danger in the corruption of morals and the wrecking of lives which they believe are caused by evil books. Obviously there will be no agreement here—just as there can be no compromise between the opponents and the supporters of capital punishment or of medical experimentation on animals. We can therefore suggest no solution whatever which all parties will accept. But at best we may make some of the issues clear.

In practice, most civilized countries exercise a close censorship over certain kinds of publications, whether their citizens hold a formulated theory of censorship or not. And in practice, most of the opponents of censorship do not believe in the indiscriminate utterance and publication of all knowledge without exception. (It is odd to hear a publisher bitterly complaining of restrictions imposed on him by a law or an organization, and then saying quite sincerely 'There were half a dozen books offered to me last year which I simply refused to touch.') Now, the fields in which practice and theory most closely coincide are the fields where knowledge passes into emotion: where acquaintance with the facts will make it difficult for irresponsible people to refrain from dangerous or wicked actions. Most people are not irresponsible. Most people have more to lose than to gain by anti-social actions: property, a job, marriage and children, the thought of illness and age, the fear of disgrace restrain them. But many young men and some girls between

6

fifteen and twenty-five, and some groups and individuals after twenty-five, are temporarily or permanently rebels. To win them over and to use their talents for their own benefit and ours, we must calm them down, divert their energies into harmless channels, commend regularity and diminish harmful excitement. Such excitement is most dangerous in three areas—sex, violence, and intoxication. Therefore it is generally thought wise to limit the free dissemination of knowledge in these areas.

Take three instances.

It would be easy to publish a book on the delights of drug-taking. Intoxication by drugs has its pleasures, some of them in placid escape from the world (as with opium addiction, coca-chewing, and the milder forms of marijuana-smoking), and others fierce and dangerous, challenging to bolder spirits. Also, the idea of belonging to a society of daring initiates often appeals to young people. Such a book need not be merely a meditation on the spiritual and aesthetic aspects of drug-taking, like Baudelaire's and De Quincey's. It would describe physical sensations in detail, discuss the comparative thrills of different types of drugs, explain the most effective methods of taking them. All this is knowledge. Ought it to be freely disseminated?

An even stronger excitement, to some minds and in some places, is cruelty and violence. There are many ingenious ways of inflicting pain on human beings and animals: Hogarth's engravings *The Progress of Cruelty* will show how much satisfaction they can give the selfish, immature, or perverted soul. To describe tortures and acts of brutality from the point of view of the torturer is certainly to make an addition to knowledge. And conversely, many millions of people have within our lifetime suffered or been threatened with atrocious acts of cruelty. Many volumes might be filled with records of them, and the records could be distributed to the victims or to the kinsmen of the victims or to those who still fear such cruelty. During the recent fighting between Sikhs, Hindus, and Moslems, many acts of unusual barbarity were committed: should albums of photographs, accompanied by detailed reports of each separate outrage, now be published in India and Pakistan? Would he who brought out such books as contributions to knowledge be a friend of mankind, or an enemy? And would the publisher of a manual of tortures, with vivid photographs and hitherto unpublished documentary statements, help or harm his fellow men?

In sexual life there are all sorts of aberrations from the usual. Most people find their most constant happiness lies in enjoying a normal sexual relationship, prepared for through their adolescence, and extending into their love for their children. But during youth, nearly everyone is tempted to commit acts and acquire habits which are by general consent degrading or foolish. One of the purposes of group discipline, in the family, the church, school and college, and society generally, is to help young people to pass through that period without too much disturbance at the time and remorse and misery later. Therefore, although it might legitimately be described as a contribution to knowledge, a book which described in full detail the stimulating effects of various abnormal and ultimately miserable types of sexual practice would be dangerous to society. A psychiatrist might well read it to understand his patients; a judge and a priest would be helped by it in administering justice and finding mercy; it is not, however, to be read by young people 'when the blood burns', and those who are already deviating from happiness ought to be shielded from it.

The huge majority of opinion in most civilized countries is, tacitly or expressly, in favour of maintaining limitations on the free publication of knowledge in these three areas at least. Whenever a new medium of communication is developed, the limitations are extended to it almost at once. It was not long after the invention of moving pictures that general agreement was reached to restrain the exhibition of films showing certain techniques of murder and torture, intoxication, drug-taking, sexual orgies, and other extremes of experience—even although they might be described as true to fact and thus as contributions to knowledge. With the appearance of radio and television the same restraints have been reaffirmed. Some think they have gone too far, some think they have not gone far enough, but scarcely anyone rejects the principle that some limitation is necessary: scarcely anyone would film a cannibal feast, however factual, and distribute it freely through public theatres, or dramatize on a national television programme one of the torture-banquets described by the Marquis de Sade. In a few important areas of life, description easily passes over into persuasion; the excitement of knowing about certain experiences soon stimulates the emotions so strongly that the entire personality may easily be altered unless it has been carefully prepared, by moral and intellectual training, to resist. St. Augustine describes how a friend of his went under protest to the greatest of Roman festivals, the games. The young man closed his eyes, in order not to see the gladiators butchering one another, the swords flashing, the blood spouting, the fall of the wounded, the triumph of the victor, and the final moment when the broad sharp blade plunged into the living flesh. But he heard a yell of excitement from the crowd all round him: he opened his eyes; and in a moment he was captured, enjoying the blood and savagery, roaring with delight at the next murder. Books have often been written in order to produce similar effects. It would be easy to write others—particularly in an era such as this, when the emotions are in many fields overpowering the intellect and when manias of various kinds are constantly spreading; and ill-disposed, greedy or maladjusted men might well write and distribute them for purposes which had nothing to do with the dissemination of knowledge.

Now, as we have said, there is no general solution to this problem: none whatever. In discussing the control of dangerous and obscene books, magazines, films, plays, and exhibitions, it is not possible to lay down a policy which everyone will accept. Citizens of the United States and of other free countries are agreed only on one principle—that there can be no general principle. Those founders of our country who wrote the First Amendment to the Constitution in 1791 made it perfectly clear:

> Congress shall make no law . . . abridging
> the freedom of speech or of the press.

This does not mean that they had infinite trust in the judgment and integrity of all writers and publishers; it does not mean that they forgot how easily and profitably the freedom of the press might be abused: they were well aware of the dangers. But they felt that any single law establishing a set of permanent rules must necessarily be inadequate. They left it to society to apply such sanctions, varying from time to time, as it thought best and wisest. Doubtless they also foresaw the growth of the republic into a huge and widely varied community, in which many different shades of opinion and levels of experience are represented: a community in which what shocks one group might be fairly considered harmless by another, so that any general prohibition might exclude some legitimate and acceptable ideas and emotions. And they knew that it was the duty of the entire nation to educate itself, morally as well as intellectually, accepting all the responsibilities of maturity.

In practice, that is what has happened. That is what is happening. Not you nor I, no single man, no group or section, has the right to tell society what it ought to accept or reject. It is the duty of all citizens to think over what is acceptable or rejectable, to weigh the consequences of accepting or rejecting, and then to make their decision known. Scarcely anyone would maintain the position that *everything* ought to be printed or exhibited, and anyone who did would find a massive force of opinion against him. Scarcely anyone would declare that society *ought* to have no standards to distinguish cruelty from mercy, lewdness from purity, moral sickness from moral health. In practice, society has such standards; and it cannot be prevented from applying them to books, any more than from applying them to other areas of public life. This does not mean that it ought to establish an official board of censors: such an institution would be at once too powerful and too weak. It does mean that every citizen has the right to be a censor for himself and his family, and in his own community in so far as he can convince them that he is talking sense. He has the right, and in fact the duty, to protest against objectionable books and exhibitions, just as he would protest against the pollution of the air and water, the adulteration of his food, or the invasion of his life by disturbers of the peace.

How he can make his protests effective—that is for him to decide. Once again, no general principle can be laid down. But it is his clear duty to ensure that his protests, as well as being effective, shall be well-informed, morally sound, and socially valuable in the broadest way. In morality, as in medicine and education, hasty action is nearly always wrong, and the ideal to aim at is that of preserving and extending a healthy equilibrium. This can be achieved only through long and responsible thinking; but such thinking is our duty. A society which draws a sharp distinction between right and wrong will live a longer and sounder life than a society which comes to believe that the difference is unimportant, and that, because some problems are too hard to solve immediately, it is not worth the trouble of thinking about them at all. One of these problems is the problem of censorship. It changes because morals change; and yet morals have a permanent basis. To determine what is permanently valuable and yet to allow for the temporary, that is the entire difficulty in accepting or rejecting books and ideas. It is difficult. It will never become easy. But it is not impossible, if we use our minds.

THE FAITH OF UNIVERSITIES

Within these special areas just described, there is pretty broad agreement in most civilized countries that restrictions on the general distribution of knowledge are necessary. But outside these, the dispute grows hot: restriction of knowledge is heartily admired and enforced in some nations, imposed against strong opposition in others, loudly resisted in others again; and it is approved or disapproved by different groups within one and the same society. All that we can do here is to reaffirm the faith held in most Western universities during the last three or four hundred years.

The faith of a Western university is that—outside the limits specified above—every responsible citizen has an absolute and inviolable right to acquire, to possess, and to publish knowledge of ascertained facts on any subject within the range of the mind.

This faith rests upon three principles, one disputed and the other two certain. These are, first, that the increase of human knowledge is good; second, that the powers of the human mind are enormous in range and ought to be more fully developed; and, third, that the best interests of every nation and of all mankind are served by the advance of knowledge. The first and the third of these principles can easily be confused, but they are not identical. It is good that we should learn more about the universe and about ourselves, even although no other benefit than our knowledge ever accrues to us and our fellow creatures. Knowledge is better than ignorance, even if that knowledge produces no further results. The man who understands the structure of a distant star-system, the man who finds an equation to describe the growth of a leaf, and the man who reveals a forgotten era of history need no further justification: their work may never be 'used'; it will still be good. Some of the discoveries made in recent research have in fact been put to uses that many wise men think evil. The discoveries remain good.

But it is the third principle which is most often challenged, especially outside the community of teachers, scholars, and students; and it is about this principle that the most serious disputes have raged for centuries.

There always have been, and there are now, many men

and women who declare that certain bodies of knowledge ought to be destroyed, or so closely restricted as to be made into secrets—not because the facts stated are false, nor because they would lead irresponsible minds into immoral conduct, but because, if widely known, they would damage some special group, or some political, religious, or social organization. There are examples of this all over the world, and more emerge every day.

During the nineteenth century the Russians attempted to abolish the Polish language and literature, forbidding it to be taught and directing that all lectures in Warsaw University be delivered in Russian; under the Germans more recently, Polish libraries were either destroyed or placed under police control. The Spanish conquerors of Mexico destroyed nearly all the historical records kept by the natives. When Galileo, working on the discoveries of Copernicus, proclaimed the fact that the earth is not the immovable centre of the universe, but is a planet revolving around the sun he was arrested, imprisoned, threatened with torture, and condemned to withdraw the statement on his knees. He withdrew it. But if he did not (as the story goes) murmur *Eppur si muove* ('It moves, all the same'), he surely said so in the recesses of his mathematical mind. In recent times the most drastic alterations of history have been undertaken for political purposes. After Stalin had won his struggle for power against Trotsky, Trotsky's work in building up the Red army was expunged from Communist history books and is now virtually forgotten inside the U.S.S.R. Such distortions are extended to quite small details. Thus, the most distinguished of modern chess masters was a Russian, Alekhine; since he repudiated the Bolshevik revolution, his name is not mentioned in Russian histories of chess.

Such actions spring from a very old human instinct. The cave man who painted a running stag and then painted a spear piercing it was not remembering something which had happened. He was making something happen. So was the Egyptian monarch who commanded that the names and titles of a magnificent predecessor should be erased from the monuments and his own names and titles substituted. If the omnipotent state planned by certain politicians ever contrives to seize control over the entire human race, its Director of Belief and Propaganda will necessarily act in the same way. After every struggle for power within the governing clique has ended, he will order all existing records to be destroyed and new records to be forged; and thus he will be creating the future by remaking the past. The aim of all such actions is to assert the authority of one particular organization: party, class, church, or dynasty.

Now, it is precisely on this point that the dispute turns. Many people—perhaps most people in the world—would rather ensure the authority of the social and religious systems to which they belong than assert the primacy of knowledge. Of all the hundreds of colleges and universities throughout the world, only a minority is devoted to the pursuit and dissemination of knowledge above all other aims. The rest are devoted to supporting authority: to bringing up young men and women as good Protestants or Catholics or Mohammedans or Communists or whatever the local pattern may be. It is from the other institutions, however, it is from the minority, that the fertilizing stream of new and newly co-ordinated knowledge has flowed: from Paris and Vienna and Berlin, from Oxford and Cambridge, Glasgow and London, Harvard and Yale and Columbia. These and a few more are the homes of the Nobel Prize winners, the sources of the great standard histories and reference works, the centres of that knowledge which, like the diamond, is tested only by itself. The faith of such a university can be put simply and boldly. It is that all human organizations pass away, but knowledge remains. To teach in such a way as to support constitutional monarchy, or the dictatorship of the National Socialist party, or the authority of the Koran, or the divine origin of the Japanese islands and people, may be valuable in a certain place for a certain time. But to establish and teach universally valid facts is to do both present and future service to the entire human race.

The difference is magnificently symbolized in one of the noblest episodes of Dante's *Comedy*. As he moves through Hell, Dante reaches a terrible region inhabited by souls that have been transmuted into living flames. These are the evil counsellors. One of them speaks, the tip of the flame flickering like a tongue. It reveals itself as the soul of the Greek prince who was the wisest of all the heroes, the explorer Ulysses; and it tells how he met his death. Even after the Trojan war and the years of wandering were over, Ulysses could not settle down. He was still dominated by his passion

> for gathering experience of the world
> and of the vice and merit of mankind.

He gathered his crew together and set out 'to sail beyond the sunset and the baths of all the western stars', exploring the mysterious ocean which we know as the Atlantic, and venturing outside the frontiers of the known world. And there, far out in the lonely inhuman waste of waters, he and his ship were suddenly struck by a storm and engulfed by a whirlpool. It was God's punishment for his insolence in exploring what was not intended for human beings to see. So Dante tells us, thinking with the mind of the Middle Ages. Yet Dante was also a universal thinker, so that he felt and understood the insatiable longing for knowledge. For the damned soul of the pagan prince he created one of the noblest exhortations ever uttered. He made Ulysses say to his sailors, as they shrank from the horror of the unknown,

> Consider well the seed from which you grew :
> you were not formed to live like animals
> but rather to pursue virtue and knowledge.

There, in a single sentence, is the faith of the Western universities.

THE FAITH APPLIED

Nevertheless, this, like other faiths, is often injudiciously applied, and distorted by unwary generalizations. It has suffered from invasion by the latest form of idol worship: the adoration of Science—not as a method of inquiry, but as a new authority, which replaces the authority of kings and churches and almost frees its worshippers from the duty of independent thought. Also, it has been over-extended by enthusiastic teachers and discoverers; and it has been corrupted simply by false logic. It is common in Communist schools to say that science has proved there is no God—an assertion as silly as saying that algebra can prove the beauty of a sunset, or chemistry the purity of a motive. Comparable blunders are made in non-Communist countries. They must be recognized and avoided.

We must distinguish fact from theory; from interpretation; from hypothesis. There are two main phases in the

work of a research scientist. One is the discovery of facts.
The other is the construction of an intellectual pattern that
will explain them in combination with other known facts.
It is the duty of the scholar and of his listeners to distinguish. They must accept proven facts; but they must realize
that interpretations are only provisional. Thus, the Nazi
experts who proclaimed that 'science' had proved the
superiority of some races to other races were talking un-
scientifically. So is anyone who asserts that Darwin's theory
of natural selection is a complete and unchallengeable
factual account of the origin of the human race and of other
species. Interpretations are not facts, and the phrase 'scientific theory' may sometimes be a contradiction in terms.

Also, facts are not judgments of value. Therefore the
scholar who discovers and teaches facts must be very wary
of assuming that they confer upon him the right to impose
any particular standards of good and evil on his pupils. The
right to knowledge must be distinguished from the right
of persuasion. A historian who explains the complicated
process by which the American or German or Spanish or
British nation reached its present condition is, in doing so,
a scholar; but the moment he adds the conclusion that all
this makes one of these nations 'the greatest nation in history', he is emitting a judgment of value. Now, part of the
duty of scholars in certain subjects is to teach people how
to make sound value judgments and to offer them certain
judgments to examine. No one would dream of teaching
English literature as though the plays of Shakespeare were
equal in interest to the plays of Noel Coward. The scholar's
duty is to give the full facts about both, and to combine
them into a firm support for the scholarly judgment that
Shakespeare's plays are better; but if some of his pupils,

knowing all the facts, still prefer Coward's, he has done all he can, and all he should. Beneath every serious dispute in the worlds of scholarship lies a judgment of value; and when that point is reached, science and scholarship must bow their heads in silence. Only one voice may still be heard: the voice of philosophy. There speaks reason. All else is only cries of emotion. Emotion is individual; transient. Reason is permanent.

It is because reason is permanent that we of the Western universities trust in it. The history of mankind shows that reason has always conquered those who try to restrict or abolish it. Again and again the attempt has been made. Again and again it has failed. It will be made again, it is being made now, and it will fail once more. The life of the human spirit faces two dangers, both appallingly powerful and urgent. One is laziness, the other is tyranny. It is perfectly possible that by the year 2000 the civilized world will have grown so rich and so comfortable, and so deeply devoted to simple asinine pleasures, that thought will be abolished, or else reserved for a few wily Managers and Experts. It is perfectly possible that education will dwindle away into nothing more than job training and courses in social and family relationships, and that life will collapse into a series of delightfully similar days, a few hours' mechanical routine followed by jolly picnics and cheap amusements. It is possible, though it is not likely. Yet, if that should happen, the unused energies of the human mind would find an outlet in spite of every comfort and every shallow distraction. There would still be inventors and researchers and thinkers, although for a few centuries they might seem as eccentric and be as rare as saints. The history of knowledge is full of the stories of such men. Every important subject begins with a few eccentrics. It is strangely encouraging to read the records of scholarship, and to see how often, while most of the world was busily engaged in the elaborate ceremonies and interminable wars of feudalism, or in the morning stag hunt, the afternoon gossip, and the evening court ball, a few men, sitting in a study or walking in a garden or reading in a library or observing and experimenting in a laboratory, were doing what really mattered, and keeping the mind of humanity alive.

It is also possible that by the year 2000 the entire planet will be subject to a total tyranny, more effective and ruthless than anything which has yet been experienced in our long history of horrors; or to several regional tyrannies.

There are two or three trends which point toward this.

The first is nationalism—the belief that one racial and political group is superior to all others and must be magnified at any cost to the individuals who compose it. The force of this belief is diminishing in some parts of the world, but elsewhere (particularly among newly-independent nations) it is growing more intense every year. Many a man whose father or grandfather thought of himself simply as X, a shopkeeper of Y-town, now sees himself exclusively as a dedicated Z-ist, ready to rush on the bayonets of all the enemies of Z-ia and to die with the glorious Z-flag wrapped around him.

The second such trend is statism, the belief that all or nearly all the activities of all the citizens of a country ought to be controlled by the government, and that such a concentration of power will not corrupt the officials to whom it is entrusted. This belief too has been growing very rapidly in the last century. It is now held more widely, perhaps, than any other theory of politics, and is often maintained with a passionate enthusiasm inversely proportioned to the understanding of its dangers. It would be amusing, if it were not painful, to watch the supporters of an intensely concentrated autocracy calling themselves 'liberal' and proclaiming that their hope is a 'new freedom'. But historians recognize the recurrence of certain emotional urges, and sadly understand that, just as men liked once to believe in the divine right of kings, they now like to believe in the the divine rightness of government officials.

Third of these trends is the advance of scientific ingenuity, making it far easier for unscrupulous men to dominate a large population through the application of technology. Machines increase power. Louis XIV had to quarter dragoons on those whom he wished to tyrannize: nowadays a concealed microphone and a few other such devices will do the same work more easily and efficiently. The Second World War was largely a scientists' war, and the possible world tyranny of the future will be, in the true sense, a scientific tyranny.

Thus, a thoroughly nationalist and state-socialist government in which officials controlled research and application in every single field of learning would be the most monumental tyranny in the history of mankind. Such a despotism has been forecast by several satirists, and has already come into existence here and there. It was established in Russia by the Bolshevik revolution; attempts to set it up in Italy and Germany were made by Mussolini and Hitler, with less durable success. George Orwell's *Nineteen Eighty-four* describes the extension of several such tyrannies over the whole world, within the lifetime of people now alive. Aldous Huxley's *Brave New World* envisages a later stage, in which, under one single planetary despotism, human beings have become mentally far more like insects. Breeding and conditioning, in that future world, are used to divide all humanity into four classes, or rather subspecies, which can scarcely even communicate with one another, but, like ants in a gigantic colony 25,000 miles in circumference, work and play and feed and copulate and never think. Such a dictatorship will be compelled by its own nature to exercise the most careful and drastic control over the minds of its subjects. It will of course prescribe everything that is to be printed in books and newspapers and magazines, everything to be heard on the radio, everything to be seen on the stage, on TV, and in films. Adolf Hitler, who in a comparatively short career took Germany far along the road to such a tyranny, said that the press was a combat weapon in the realm of thought comparable to the airplane in warfare. 'Today', he boasted, 'the [Nazi] journalist knows that he is no mere scribbler, but a man with the sacred mission of defending the highest interests of the [Nazi] state.' The dictatorship will be forced to suppress critical books which might encourage opposition. But also it will conceal facts, destroy records, prohibit research and teaching in certain areas, and try to reduce all thinking men to intellectual serfs of the all-powerful state, instead of allowing them to obey the only universally acceptable master under God, human reason. It will cause a great deal of misery in the process, waste many valuable lives, and inevitably damage its own interests by refusing to use the best of men's powers.

In the end it will fail. It is not possible to dehumanize all mankind. Someone will be left, thinking. The governing clique itself must continue to think, and as each generation of children is born, new thinkers will appear. It would be easier to destroy mankind physically, with a germ

7

or an explosion, than to destroy it mentally. For men are frail, and panicky, and subject to intermittences of health and emotion; but they are adaptable, and their adaptability means constant ability to change and develop the powers of their mind. They have emerged, within a few score thousand generations, from the jungles and the caves, by thinking and by changing. As long as men live upon this planet, they will, they must, continue to think; and they will think in spite of the worst tyrannies and cruelties that they can devise for one another.

Strange, unfathomable happiness: the happiness of thinking, of seeking knowledge for its own sake. So much of our life is spent on solving problems to avoid immediate pain or to bring immediate profit; so much of our training is aimed at bringing 'practical' or 'pragmatic' effects, designing and running machines, buying, selling, cooking, furnishing, investing, spending; so many worthy results are obtained by purposeful planning and directed thinking—that we forget how true and inexhaustible is the happiness of pure knowing. Everyone has tasted it. It is born in children. It goes to school with them, and is too often killed there by tired or 'practical' teachers. But in some it survives, and unlike other delights it endures for the whole of life. To spend fifty or sixty years in studying the structure of fishes, or the relation between logic and language, or the history of the Incas, or the routes of comets, or the geometry of non-Euclidean space, or the literature of Iceland, or the anatomy of the brain; to acquire and systematize and record new knowledge on any of these subjects without any expectation of benefiting mankind except by extending its range of understanding: that is to pass a happy and valuable life, usually tempered at the close by regret that another fifty years could not be added, in which to learn more, and still more. It is the purest and least selfish satisfaction known to man, except those of creating a work of art and healing the sick. And it is, as Aristotle said, to share the activity of God himself: his eternal life of pure contemplation.

CHAPTER NINE

Inherent Limitations of the Mind

YET we are not gods. No, nor godlike, except by glimpses—in moments when we see a little of the truth, or do a little good. We are imperfect. We are inadequate. Morally, almost all religions start by assuming that we are far from successful. Intellectually, almost all philosophers agree that we are often mistaken and always weak.

Many acute observers of the human mind have earned a place in history by doubting its powers. Such was the Portuguese Jew, Francisco Sanchez, who in 1581 published a brilliant book with the simple title *Quod Nihil Scitur* (Nothing Can Be Known). Such was the mild and humorous essayist, Michel de Montaigne, who spent long years endeavouring to comprehend himself, and who symbolized his thinking by the emblem of a pair of scales and the motto *Que Sçay-Je?* And such too was the Roman officer who asked Jesus one of the few questions that Jesus never answered. After examining Jesus, he found him guiltless; but when Jesus said he was born 'to bear witness unto the truth', Pontius Pilate asked 'What is truth?'

INCOMPLETENESS OF SENSES AND MIND

No one can think effectively without admitting the inherent limitations of the mind. To begin with, our senses are few and their range is small. Only two of them (sight and touch) really help us to extend our knowledge. Throughout the world interesting and important things are happening which our senses do not report, which they cannot possibly report. Waves and currents of energy are incessantly flowing through our surroundings and even our bodies: we neither see nor hear nor feel them. One of the principal aims of the sciences is to extend the range of our limited senses by making us more powerful eyes to look through, or by translating invisible and inaudible phenomena into events that can be heard or seen.

More important is the fact that the structure of the mind itself is limited. Obviously, individual minds have individual inadequacies: one cannot understand symbols, another has no verbal agility. But *every* human mind is drastically limited. That is the essence of the philosophy of Immanuel Kant. He demonstrated—not altogether simply, but finally —that the human intellect is compelled by its own structure to arrange its experiences in certain restricted ways, fitting them into patterns of space and time, although the flow of events may be experienced by other minds in quite different patterns. Necessarily, we can experience only a fraction of the total movement of events.

IMPOSSIBILITY OF CERTAIN TYPES OF KNOWLEDGE

Further, certain important types of knowledge are by nature incomplete or impossible. Our knowledge of ourselves is always imperfect. Our knowledge of the divine is always inadequate.

For many centuries, astute men and women have been

watching themselves and others: in education and religion and politics, in literature and social life and in various types of psychological study. They have nearly all agreed that it is virtually impossible to know the minds of other people and extremely hard even to understand one's own. Not one of us can predict what his nearest relative, or even he himself, will do in critical moments. Not one of us can forecast the future development of his own mind and character. Political history, from one point of view, is a long series of bad guesses and shocking surprises. Group psychology is outrageously difficult. Individual psychology is virtually impossible. Of course psychology may develop in the future, as copiously and satisfyingly as medicine has done during the past 500 years. We cannot tell. So far, it knows hardly anything about the activities of the mind.

Metaphysical knowledge, although even more important, is equally difficult. For some of us it has been made easier by revelations proceeding from God through a Mediator or Apostle; but even such revelations are limited in scope, saying nothing of many questions which concern us vitally as soon as we start thinking. I suppose there are not a hundred men in the history of mankind who have ever understood time. Very few have fathomed the connection of body and spirit. Very few have been able to explain what death is. And as for the nature of God—it is almost by definition inexpressible, incomprehensible, the Absolute. We know that There Is. We do not know What Is.

INADEQUACY OF THE SCIENCES

But surely we are not condemned to perpetual ignorance? Surely Science will help us toward complete understanding?

No. There are naive people all over the world—some of them scientists—who believe that all problems, sooner or later, will be solved by Science. The word Science itself has become a vague reassuring noise, with a very ill-defined meaning and a powerful emotional charge: it is now applied to all sorts of unsuitable subjects and used as a cover for careless and incomplete thinking in dozens of fields. But even taking Science at the most sensible of its definitions, we must acknowledge that it is as imperfect as all other activities of the human mind.

There is no such thing as Science. There are only sciences, departments of knowledge acquired in a special way. They do not always agree. On several important subjects they do not even meet, far less cohere. Very few men in the entire world understand more than the outlines of all the sciences. No one has ever grouped all their reports together into a single experience of the universe. That may be done in the future, because most of the human mind is still unused, and in particular its power to assemble, to make syntheses, can be far more richly developed. But even then it will be an intellectual effort of which few men and women will be capable. The sciences report facts to ordinary men. It takes a great man to understand them.

> Flower in the crannied wall,
> I pluck you out of the crannies,
> I hold you here, root and all, in my hand,
> Little flower—but *if* I could understand
> What you are, root and all, and all in all,
> I should know what God and man is.

Beyond science—

It is a humbling experience to walk through the shelves

of a big university library. There they stand, books by the hundreds, by the thousands and hundreds of thousands, shelf after shelf, tier upon tier, with a constant inflow of new books edging the old books to the wall or thrusting them into the cellars. No human being has read them all. No human being could. No human being can even master half of the subjects which they cover. Sociology, Persian dialects, the history of the stage, biochemistry, jurisprudence, seismology, optics, the theory of banking, astrophysics, comparative religion—the list is wonderful, but it is discouraging. It was only in the confident eras that men could profess to know all that was knowable and to organize it: St. Thomas Aquinas in the Middle Ages, the Admirable Crichton in the Renaissance, and in Greece 'the master of those who know', the wisest of all mankind, Aristotle. But then such knowledge was at best a hope. Now it is clearly an impossibility. And often, as one walks among the shelves, glancing at books with bold and rewarding titles, one wishes at least the wish of the scholar, if not the saint: one prays not for eternity, but for more time.

But it is all inadequate. The books are solid. The books are valuable. The books are 'scientific'. But everyone knows —even their authors know—that they are incomplete. All the work of the mind is inadequate. In understanding the world, our lives, and ourselves, other methods are needed also, and they are frequently superior to anything we can call intellectual.

EXPERIENCE BEYOND KNOWLEDGE

Every man, however dull and unimaginative or however efficient and rational his life may be, finds experiences of all kinds flooding in upon him from sources and through channels which are not intellectual at all. They are powerful experiences, part of the total flux of reality. But they cannot be called 'knowledge' in the accepted sense. They lie outside the frontiers of knowledge. The mystics constantly tell us this. The artists show it to us in wonderful shapes and colours, not to be apprehended by the intellect. This truth is at the heart of music. We all possess it, but—at least in Western countries—we too often conceal it from ourselves.

Most clearly and powerfully, this is displayed by music. To sit in a quiet room as evening falls, and to hear four stringed instruments discoursing among themselves in a miraculous variety of wordless speech, sounds that laugh and dance or weep and mourn or argue briskly or compete urgently and exist separately but also enjoy a harmonious life in common; or, in a concert hall, to surrender with a thousand others to the massive energy of Beethoven's spirit, miraculously reincarnated in a moving tide of sound that flows from fifty instruments and for half an hour dominates time and change; or, perhaps best of all, to sit alone at a piano, to play one of the fugues of Bach and to feel that calm and searching mind speaking through one's own fingers, uttering truths one could never grasp by oneself and disciplining one's very soul to an intenser contemplation and a loftier serenity—that is to realize that much experience, and much of the best experience, lies altogether beyond knowledge.

Yes, all the arts have meanings, and their meanings are not to be grasped by rational thought. A good poem, a fine play, the movements of a dancer, cannot be explained. The Japanese who paints a pine branch covered with thick powdery snow, or the Mexican who changes a stone slab into a monstrous deity, is making a statement about the universe; but the statement cannot be translated into intellectual terms. The great myths of every culture are such statements, and so are the rituals which often accompany them. They give shape and authority to unreason. In the delightful image of a delightful poet, Ralph Hodgson,

> Reason has moons, but moons not hers
> Lie mirrored on the sea,
> Confounding her astronomers,
> But, O! delighting me.

Experience of truth beyond knowledge is gained by everyone, at some time in his life, from two far more primitive and fundamental sources: from physical activity and from the love of nature. Some of the earliest paintings of human beings that we have yet discovered show them in groups, dancing and clapping their hands. One can almost, over the gap of fifty thousand years, hear the drums; and as one gazes one's heart begins to beat in a stronger rhythm. Great poets have loved the sea, and swum for hours among rough surges, or, sailing in small boats, felt the wind and the waves become part of their being. Wise and happy men have loved a good horse, and taken delight in riding hour after hour through forest paths, in silence, but constantly aware of some incommunicable truth. Throughout history, since God Almighty first planted a garden, we have loved and understood growing things and beasts and birds. Throughout history, we have revered and tried to understand the tempests and the tides, the rain and the sunlight. The smallest and the greatest things in nature are equally full of wonder and of meaning. It is an equally deep experience to gaze at a gull riding the wind, a butterfly imitating a leaf, or a river plunging down a precipice. And there are many men who have felt that, at last, without the work of the busy human mind, they have been able to comprehend some of the greatest secrets of the universe, when, after climbing all day through the pine trees and then sitting for an hour by a lonely fire on the dark mountainside, they have lain down to sleep on the huge body of the earth among the cool breath of the peaks, and then, in the morning, watched the sun rise as gloriously as on the day of creation.

Last, there is one central area of all experience that lies, in the main, beyond the scope of rational understanding. This is morality and religion. Again and again the great teachers tell us that wisdom and goodness are not the same, and that the truths of religion are not to be apprehended by reason. Again and again we forget. Again and again, clever men and women endeavour to reduce ethics to a mathematical scheme or a legal formula and to abolish the absurdities of religion by denying worship to the worshipful. Again and again, their hearts break unexpectedly: they find themselves on their knees. As Browning's ambitious priest says,

> Just when we're safest, there's a sunset-touch,
> A fancy from a flower-bell, someone's death,
> A chorus-ending from Euripides,
> And that's enough for fifty hopes and fears,
> As old and new at once as nature's self,
> To rap and knock and enter in our soul,
> Take hands and dance there, a fantastic ring,
> Round the ancient idol, on his base again,
> The grand Perhaps!

This is one of the truths that Jesus came to bear witness to. It is instructive to watch him, in discussion with the astute intelligentsia of Jewry, driving it home with over-powering emphasis. They kept coming to him and asking him hard questions, in the hope that they could prove him either ignorant of the Scriptures (in particular, of all their legal and ritual niceties) or else an immoralist. Occasionally he would counter-attack with painful queries of his own which they could not answer; but usually he soared above the dilemma on the wings of a noble, simple, mystical utterance which silenced them and became an immortal statement of a truth not to be reached through reason alone.

There is a strange little prose poem by a famous Frenchman. It is a prayer on the Acropolis, the central citadel of Athens, addressed to the goddess Athena, the personification of calm reason. Its author, Ernest Renan, was trained as a Roman Catholic priest, but abandoned the priesthood. Poor, ambitious, industrious, clever, he made himself into one of the foremost scholars of the nineteenth century, specializing in the languages and history of the Near East. His chief works were a history of the people of Israel and a history of the origins of Christianity. Both were written from intimate knowledge of Israel and the lands around it, from profound study of the Bible and other sources of evidence, and evidently from a warm sympathy, an affection which refused to be transformed into adoration, for Jesus and his followers, for the Jewish kings and prophets, and for the Hebrew people themselves. But the purpose of his writings was to abolish the divinity of Christ, to deny the validity of Christianity as a universal religion, and to reduce much of the spiritual history of the Judaeo-Christian world to a series of emotional adventures far inferior to the steady work of the human reason. His own creed? His own creed was never publicly stated, except perhaps in his *Prayer on*

Foresighted, the Searcher. As the drama opens, he is being nailed to a crag in the desolate Caucasus mountains by two monsters, Power and Violence. They are agents of the supreme being, God or Zeus. They are punishing him for seeking out secrets that God wished to keep inviolate, and for giving them to mankind for its welfare. Like Job among the ashes, Prometheus inflexibly declares that he cannot accept undeserved suffering, that he will not be reconciled, that God is unjust. Other victims of God's cruelty visit him. At last he is offered a reconciliation if he will submit to the divinity and assist his reign. He refuses. He clings to his own reason and to the liberty of his spirit. The earth opens, carrying the crucified hero down to torments still more frightful, an eternity of hell.

And yet the myth does not end there. By a bitter chance, we have lost the play which Aeschylus wrote to follow *Prometheus Bound*. Somewhere in the Dark Ages of war and barbarism, the last manuscript of this masterpiece was torn up by a disappointed looter, or burnt in a devastated library, or (like its hero) swallowed up in a cataclysmic earthquake. But we know something of it; and we know that, by his transcendent genius, the poet showed a final reconciliation between reason and deity, between Prometheus and Zeus. When reason fails to harmonize with the other forces that make up reality, there is tragedy; that is the tragedy which somehow Aeschylus contrived to solve, as the final poet of the Book of Job also solved it. Through what marvellous re-creation and combination of mythical truths Aeschylus found a solution, we cannot now tell. Certain it is that, out of the apparently endless discord between knowledge and the remainder of experience, he drew a majestic harmony, such harmony as is in immortal souls.

CHAPTER ELEVEN

Necessity

WITH all its limitations, with all its dangers, reason is still one of the essential powers of man. It is not his sole essence. He is not a thinking machine, nor should he try to become one. He is not a thinking animal. He is something much more, something greater and more complex. 'How noble in reason!' says the greatest of poets, and goes on 'how infinite in faculty!' before adding one more of his inimitable, unforgettable phrases, 'this quintessence of dust'. But thinking is one of the necessary activities that make him human. He must think.

Day and night, from childhood to old age, sick or well, asleep or awake, men and women think. The brain works like the heart, ceaselessly pulsing. In its three pounds' weight of tissue are recorded and stored billions upon billions of memories, habits, instincts, abilities, desires and hopes and fears, patterns and tinctures and sounds and inconceivably delicate calculations and brutishly crude urgencies, the sound of a whisper heard thirty years ago, the resolution impressed by daily practice for fifteen thousand days, the hatred cherished since childhood, the delight never experienced but incessantly imagined, the complex structure of stresses in a bridge, the exact pressure of a single finger on a single string, the development of ten thousand different games of chess, the precise curve of a lip, a hill, an equation, or a flying ball, tones and shades and glooms and raptures, the faces of countless strangers, the scent of one garden, prayers, inventions, crimes, poems, jokes, tunes, sums, problems unsolved, victories long past, the fear of Hell and the love of God, the vision of a blade of grass and the vision of the sky filled with stars.

It is curious to be awake and watch a sleeper. Seldom, when he awakes, can he remember anything of his sleep. It is a dead part of his life. But watching him, we know he was alive, and part of his life was thought. His body moved. His eyelids fluttered, as his eyes saw moving visions in the darkness. His limbs sketched tiny motions, because his sleeping fancy was guiding him through a crowd, or making him imagine a race, a fight, a hunt, a dance. He smiled a little, or looked anxious, or turned angrily from one side to the other. Sometimes (like Lord Byron) he ground his teeth in rage, and still slept. Sometimes he spoke, in a scarcely articulate shout or a gentle murmur sounding strong in his mind. His heart beat fast with excitement, or slow with despair. He sweated. He felt the passage of time and was making himself ready for the morning with its light and noise. And all that time he was thinking—vaguely and emotionally if he was intellectually untrained, in symbols, animals, and divinities if he was a primitive man, often in memories, sometimes in anticipations of the future, and, far oftener than he himself would believe, forming intricate and firm decisions on difficult problems carried over from his waking life. He will say 'I never dream, I only sleep'; but he arises with eight hours of thought written on the records of his brain as surely as another strain of grey has grown on his hair or a new firmness in the muscles of his shoulder. He may call the result a vision or a determination, a revelation or a whim, but it is a thought, worked out by his brain while he slept as surely as his heart was beating and his pancreas secreting digestive juices. Awake or asleep, man thinks. Sometimes it seems as though the chief distinction between powerful and ineffective men lay in the control and direction of their thoughts: the wise and energetic man contrives to use his mind even while his body sleeps, the stupid and helpless man dreams half his life away, even when his eyes are open. Almost every man of affairs acknowledges this when he says 'That is a difficult decision: I'll sleep on it.' Poincaré the mathematician knew it well. Just before going to sleep, he wrote down his hardest problems, and often woke with them solved, clarified during the night hours by his unsleeping brain.

Day and night, throughout their entire lives, men think. They think as naturally and inevitably as they breathe. It is a crime to deny them the best material for thought, as it is a crime to deprive them without just cause of health, liberty, and life. And it is one of their duties to themselves to think as copiously and richly as they can, to exercise and enjoy their minds as they exercise and enjoy their bodies, making them part of the total harmony which is their life.

Anthropologists sometimes seem to talk as though they believed it impossible to compare one society with another, calling one 'superior' and another 'inferior'. Yet they would agree, like the rest of us, that a nation whose children died in infancy or grew up weak and sickly was inferior physically to a nation which kept its children alive and contrived for them a long and healthy life. In the same way there can

be no doubt that a superior nation is one which uses the
minds of its people, giving them a constant flow of interesting ideas to think about, ensuring that no class or group is
kept from acquiring knowledge because of sex, colour, caste,
religion, or poverty, stimulating the free fresh production of
ideas, respecting those who record and transmit knowledge,
keeping open many channels of communication within the
frontiers of the country, and beyond them throughout the
world, and not only across geographical distances but
through the long ranges of historical time. There have been
too few nations such as that. It is for that encouragement of
knowledge, that fertility and interchange of ideas, that we
admire republican Athens, Augustan Rome, Renaissance
Italy, and the France, England, and Germany of the nineteenth century. It is sad, nevertheless, to think through
history, and to see how many millions of men and women,
in so many hundreds of societies, have lived and died ignorant and thought-benumbed, as though born deaf and blind.

> Knowledge to their eyes her ample page
>   Rich with the spoils of time did ne'er unroll;
> Chill penury repressed their noble rage
>   And froze the genial current of the soul.

It is sobering to think that we ourselves, our children or
their children, might be thrust into the same numbness, imprisoned in the narrow limits of daily routine, or suffering,
or (even worse) pleasure. Against such dangers we must
constantly assert the right to knowledge, its free possession
and use.

CHAPTER TWELVE

Responsibility

THE right to knowledge cannot be exercised for the whole people by any single group or preserved in any one institution. During the worst days of Hitler's war, those who were concerned with keeping resistance and the spirit of independence alive among the subjugated countries found that it was most difficult to do so in those nations which were most simply organized, and easiest in those which possessed many diverse organs of thought and expression —trade unions, village councils, leisure-time societies, different types of schools, colleges, universities, and technical institutes, women's clubs, social and aesthetic associations, independent newspapers and publishing houses, professional groups, and so forth. In the same way, the spread and vitality of knowledge in a free society is best assured by the lively interest of many different types of association within it. It is good that there should be competing types of school. It is good that trade unions and workers' clubs should sponsor the education of their members. Better a dozen local independent papers than a hundred news-sheets printed from a single master copy sent down from the big city. Better a county association of amateur naturalists than a course of radio lectures by a single 'eminent authority'. Freedom of knowledge, like other freedoms, rests on many different pillars and is unsafe on one or two alone. Thinking is everyone's business.

Yet knowledge is power, and power entails responsibility. The free use of knowledge is a dangerous or a meaningless phrase unless it connotes—like all liberties—activity controlled by responsibility. The darkest pages of our history books are filled with the records of men who acquired vast knowledge and used it utterly without scruple; and, as human control over techniques and mechanical power increases, we shall see many more such men. There are very few types of knowledge that cannot be used to hurt someone.

We have already considered the limitations which are by fairly general consent imposed on the use of knowledge. They can be reduced to a single principle—a principle that contains both the truth which most of us accept and the problem by which most of us are, from time to time, sorely puzzled. The principle is simply that knowledge must not be used to hurt human beings; and the difficulty is to determine which human beings we must endeavour to serve and to protect.

To this problem the simplest answer is the boldest and the broadest. It is that we must think of all humanity. And that means not only the planet-load of 2,200,000,000 people now alive. It means the myriad myriad men and women of the future; it means also the achievements of the men and women of the past, who still live around us in noble institutions and great buildings and magnificent books and splendid inventions. Of course, it is most often through serving one's own group that one can benefit mankind. A nation, a profession, a creed often commands all one's loyalty because it contributes irreplaceable values to the sum of human happiness. But the duty of everyone in acquiring and using his knowledge is to make very sure that in doing so he does not injure the welfare of mankind. The government official who suppresses a controversial book, the 'progressive' teacher who cuts down the sciences or throws the

classics out of school and college—these men are destroying
the achievement of the past and damaging the inheritance
of the future exactly as though they were defacing a famous
painting, pouring acid on a noble statue, or burning the
records of a historic event. The present does not exist. Only
the past and the future exist, and we have a duty to them
both.

It is to help each new generation to understand and
perform this duty that colleges and universities are maintained. They do not always succeed, because human enterprises are necessarily imperfect. But they try. There were
many such institutions in the world of Greece and Rome
—beginning with the Academy where Plato taught, and
the Lyceum founded by his pupil Aristotle. When the western empire collapsed and the savages flooded in, scarcely
one of those homes of learning survived; and those which
did were soon closed by intolerant monarchs. Knowledge
was kept precariously alive only here and there in a tiny
medical school, a lonely monastery, a half-literate king's
court. But then, after the year 1000, colleges and universities began to appear again throughout western and central
Europe—some almost spontaneously in cities where many
strangers met, some around famous teachers, some founded
by a generous donor or a wise bishop. Paris, Oxford, Sala-
manca, Bologna, Cracow, Glasgow, Prague, they sprang up
one by one, exchanging knowledge and arguments, pitting
their best scholars against one another, and growing in a
springlike fervour of the intellect. In North and Central and
South America, a few years after the European settlers
landed, they were founding new universities on the model
of those they knew: St. Mark's in Peru, the University of
Mexico, near which the earliest American books were

printed, and Harvard—named after a young divine who once studied with John Milton, and first stocked with books he brought from Cambridge University to the New World. Throughout these last centuries, the universities of Europe and America have nobly justified the hopes of those who founded them, and have nobly served all mankind. Honour to them. Honour to those who created them and have maintained them. They are one of the central strengths of our civilization.

CHAPTER THIRTEEN

Dedication

To feel the strength and enjoy the wealth of that tradition is one of the student's chief rewards.

Among the trees of Oxford stands a laboratory, quiet and unpretentious: there Florey and his team perfected penicillin. In central Berlin there is a battered mansion, once a royal palace and later a great university: one wing of it still remembers the hasty step and the high voice of the master historian Mommsen. An old panelled room glows with the gold sunlight of Montpellier: Rabelais lectured there on Greek medicine and modern anatomy, and his portrait still looks gravely down from the wall. There is an austere barrack in Paris, busy, ugly, noisy; but it is the Ecole Normale Supérieure: Pasteur is only one of a host of brilliant minds who have worked and taught there. Within this placid building at Yale the cool logical mind of Gibbs elaborated the laws of thermodynamics. That Harvard staircase, creaking and echoing, once rang with the strong voice of Kittredge, most robust of all interpreters of literature. And here, among the highest roofs of Columbia, there still burn the laboratory lights by which, exploring the mysteries of a world too subtle for human senses, Rabi completed the intricate and imaginative calculations that brought him the Nobel Prize.

Even to tread the floor of such a room, knowing no more than the outlines of the work done there, is to forget one's own petty self, to revere the ardours and efforts of the great thinkers and teachers who have helped to make our world, and to feel, like the majestic roll of some vast river, the urgent march of the mind, imperfect but marvellous, unique in every individual and yet super-personal, the mysterious power which has brought us out of bestial savagery toward civilization and wisdom, and will take us further still. It is to dedicate oneself again to the purpose of the university, which is to acquire and to extend knowledge for the service of all mankind.

NOTES

3 one of the noblest of Greek tragedies/ *Antigone,* by Sophocles. The quotation contains lines 332-41, 354-60, and 365-67.

10 in a very few regions/ See N. I. Vavilov, *The Origin, Variation, Immunity, and Breeding of Cultivated Plants,* translated by K. S. Chester, in *Chronica Botanica,* Vol. XIII (1949-50). For qualifications drawn from archaeological research see C. D. Forde, *Habitat, Economy, and Society* (6th ed., London, 1950).

12 'misfortunes of mankind'/ Gibbon, *Decline and Fall of the Roman Empire,* Chap. 3 (Everyman edition, I, 77).

14 Nietzsche/ See his *Geburt der Tragödie aus dem Geiste der Musik,* § 2.

15 *Paideia: The Ideals of Greek Culture,* translated by Gilbert Highet (Oxford, Blackwell, 1939-44).

17 through a mistranslation/ 'Testament' is a poor translation of *diathéké,* the Hebrew *berit,* which means 'Covenant': the idea being that God made two covenants with mankind, one through Abraham and the Jews, the other through Jesus and Christianity. See, for instance, *Dictionnaire de théologie catholique,* XV (Paris, 1950) 182-86.

17 Dante's *Comedy/* See W. H. V. Reade, *The Moral System of Dante's Inferno* (Oxford, 1909), Chap. 23.

18 balance of powers/ Formulated and described by Polybius (*c.*203-*c.*120 B.C.) in his analysis of the strength of the rising Roman Republic: see his *History* 6.11-18.

18 brotherhood of man/ See, for instance, Marcus Aurelius, *Meditations* 9.9 and 11.8.

19 covered with libraries/ See C. H. Roberts, 'Literature and Society in the Papyri', *Museum Helveticum,* X (1953), 264-79.

19 mayor of Ephesus/ Acts xix. 35-41.

19 Athenian intelligentsia/ Acts xvii. 18-33.

19 'no man forbidding him'/ Acts xxviii. 30-31.

21 close to magic/ The word *glamour,* meaning magical power, is simply another form of *grammar,* the knowledge of reading and writing.

24 from contemporary Asia/ See R. E. Pipes, 'Russian Moslems before and after the Revolution', in *Soviet Imperialism: Its Origins and Tactics,* edited by W. Gurian (Notre Dame, Indiana, 1953), pp. 75-89, esp. 87-88.

30 I trust, too/ John Masefield, *Odtaa* (London, Heinemann, 1926), p. 416.

32 'a foot to his height?'/ Matt. vi. 27.

37 *into Chapman's Homer/* S. Colvin, *John Keats* (London, 1920), pp. 38-41.

38 signed with their honour/ Stephen Spender, *Poems* (2nd ed., London, Faber, 1934), p. 30.

42 Vannevar Bush/ 'As We May Think', in *Endless Horizons* (Washington, 1946), esp. pp. 32-35.

46 the mass of men was as well qualified for flying as for thinking/ Swift, 'The Letter: Mr. Collins's Discourse of Free-thinking', in *Writings on Religion and the Church,* edited by Temple Scott (London, 1898), I, 182.

48 lost golf balls/ T. S. Eliot, 'The Rock', *Collected Poems,* 1909-1935 (London, Faber, 1936), p. 103.

50 buries all/ Pope, *The Dunciad,* 4.640, 649-56.

52 'of the Ephesians!'/ Acts xix. 34.

52 'from the earth!'/ Acts xxii. 22.

53 *The Captive Mind/* By Czeslaw Milosz, translated by Jane Zielonko (New York, Knopf, 1953).

54 speak to him/ Job i-ii.

54 meaningless or cruel/ Job iii, vi-vii, x, xix.

54 calls for a reason/ Job xxiii-xxiv.

55   back into silence/ Job xxxi. 40, ending the central debate between Job and his friends.

55   is soon stilled/ Elihu's arguments (Job xxxii-xxxvii) are much shallower than the rest of the poem. Elihu does not appear anywhere outside this single monologue, to which neither Job, nor his friends, nor the Almighty makes any reference. Therefore he was obviously invented by an orthodox writer after the main body of the poem had been written, and his words were stuck on like a plaster over Job's sores.

55   of a mighty storm/ Job xxxviii. 1-xli. 34.

56   with his sons?/ Job xxxviii. 31-32.

56   nest on high?/ Job xxxix. 26-27. The strange poetry of Job xli looks like an evocation of the terrible inhabitants of the prehistoric world, the monstrous lizards who ruled the earth for fifty million years.

56   mine eye seeth thee/ Job xlii. 3, 5.

57   praise and prayer/ The core of the book is the debate between Job and his friends, iii-xxxi. To this have been added the monologue of Elihu (xxxii-xxxvii) and the magnificent speech of God with Job's answer (xxxviii-xlii. 6). The introduction and the happy ending are in prose, different in conception and execution.

58   'swims into his ken'/ Keats, *On First Looking into Chapman's Homer*.

60   by poverty depress'd/ Johnson, *London* 176, adapted from Juvenal, 3.164-65.

61   'belongs her calf'/ See J. T. Fowler's edition of Adamnan's *Vita S. Columbae* (Oxford, 1920), p. 55.

63   every Brahmin boy/ See Gardner Murphy, *In the Minds of Men* (New York, Basic Books, 1953), Chap. 6, especially pp. 104-6.

70   necessary limitations of the right to knowledge/ Any realistic discussion of this subject is bound to recognize the differences between principle and practice. Similar differences occur in the question of religious toleration. Many Western countries uphold the principle that all religious faiths should be tolerated. But in practice none of them would tolerate a faith which, like many religions, involved human sacrifice; or, like one once widespread form of Hinduism, commanded

widows to be burned alive; or, like early Mormonism, enjoined polygamy; or, like scores of cults all over the world, was based on the
ritual torture of animals and men.

73 'when the blood burns'/ *Hamlet* 1.3.116.

74 St. Augustine/ *Confessions* 6.8.

79 kept by the natives/ C. S. Braden, *Religious Aspects of the
Conquest of Mexico* (Durham, N.C., 1930), p. 166.

79 histories of chess/ So says Kenneth Matthews, *British Chess*
(London, 1948), p. 12.

80 of one particular organization/ Probably the oldest, and certainly
the most highly organized, system of censorship is that maintained
by the Roman Catholic Church and administered by the Congregation
of the Holy Office, once better known as the Inquisition. The church
began to condemn books as soon as the Roman Emperors granted
toleration to the Christian religion. The first to be formally banned
was *Thalia,* by the priest Arius, who was judged heretical at the
Council of Nicaea in A.D. 325. Similar condemnations were made
throughout the Middle Ages.
  In 1467, soon after the invention of printing, the pope Innocent
VIII ordered all books to be examined by church authorities before
publication, and forbade the issue of any book lacking such approval.
Later, after the Reformation, the Council of Trent (1545-63) set up
a general catalogue of forbidden books, confirmed Innocent VIII's
ruling, and added nine regulations describing books which were auto-
matically prohibited because of their contents. The present censorship
policy of the church is described in the code of canon law introduced
in 1918.
  The Index itself actually names several thousand individual books
and some 120 individual authors; but the list of names is not a general
register of all books disapproved by the Roman Catholic church. It is
rather a collection of names on which, at the request of some Roman
Catholic, special pronouncements have been made. Therefore it appears rather unsystematic and is full of surprises. It includes the
complete works of Croce, Maeterlinck, Zola, Hobbes, Hume, Descartes
(as a philosopher), Gide, and Sartre; also the entire dictionary of
Larousse, *Mein Kampf* is not on the list, but Milton's *State Papers* are.
Darwin's *Origin of Species* does not appear, but Bacon's *Advancement
of Learning* does. (Only four American authors are explicitly banned:
J. W. Draper, G. Zurcher, T. Smyth-Vaundry, and W. Y. Sullivan,
obscure anti-Catholic or rationalist writers now long forgotten.)
  However, a much broader prohibition covers certain classes of lit-

erature which are condemned en bloc. This canon covers all books defending atheism, materialism, divorce, suicide, duelling, abortion, or contraception; 'professedly discussing, describing, or teaching impure and obscene matters'; denying the divine inspiration of the Bible. And it forbids any book on religion by any author who is not a Roman Catholic 'unless it is certain that it contains nothing contrary to the Catholic religion'. Obviously this must rule out hundreds of thousands of books.

It is understood that students, teachers, librarians, editors, and other persons whose interest in prohibited books is seriously justifiable may be given permission to read and possess forbidden works. But explicitly obscene and anti-Roman Catholic books are apparently excluded even from such a relaxation of the ban; and it seems to be left to the discretion of the local authorities to grant or withhold permission in every individual case.

It is needless to ask whether the Roman Catholic or any other church has the right to make such rules for its members. Every group which has the right to exist has the right to make its own rules. What is not generally admitted is the right of the Roman Catholic or any other church to impose such rules on men and women who do not belong to it—either in principle, by threatening them with penalties for reading such works, or in practice, by dissuading booksellers and libraries from handling them. Ultimately this is a religious and philosophical question. The members of the Roman Catholic church believe that it alone possesses the truth, divinely revealed, so that those who differ from it are in error, as though they declared the square root of 9 was 2. And further, they believe that the accepted Roman Catholic writers can never be shown to be wrong: it is possible to uphold Aristotle against Plato or vice versa, but never possible to uphold Pelagius against St. Augustine or Abelard against St. Bernard. Unless I am gravely mistaken, this belief is based on the conception that the Roman Catholic church (and it alone) is the representative of Jesus himself as a teacher, and is therefore literally unable to teach what is false; or, more loftily, that the Roman Catholic church as the Mystical Body of Christ is the incarnation of God, God himself alive and working on this earth: so that whenever a church authority pronounces a judgment, it proceeds not from a human mind but from the mind of God. Evidently these conceptions are so mystical that they can hardly be discussed by logic alone, and they are accepted by very few persons who are not Roman Catholics.

The figures in this note, and other data, are taken from a recent work by a Roman Catholic librarian: *What is the Index?* by R. A. Burke (Milwaukee, 1952). It has a useful bibliography.

81 Dante's *Comedy*/ See *Inferno* 26, esp. 97-99 and 118-20.

81 'all the western stars'/ Tennyson, *Ulysses* 60-61.

86 G. Orwell, *Nineteen Eighty-four* (London, 1949).

86 H. Huxley, *Brave New World* (London, 1932).

87 'of the [Nazi] state'/ *Hitler's Table Talk,* edited by H. R. Trevor-Roper (London, 1953).

89 pure contemplation/ Aristotle, *Nicomachean Ethics* 10.7-8 (1177a12-1179a32, esp. 1178b7-24).

89 not gods/ In spite of Genesis iii. 22.

89 *Que Sçay-je?* appears in Montaigne's *Apologie de Raymond Sebond* on p. 145 at line 4075 of the edition by P. Porteau (Paris, 1937). On Sanchez, see F. Strowski, *Montaigne* (Paris, 1931), Chap. 4.

89 'What is truth?'/ John xviii. 37-38. The story is not in Matt. xxvii, Mark xv, or Luke xxiii.

92 what God and man is/ Tennyson, *Flower in the Crannied Wall.*

93 'those who know'/ Dante, *Inferno* 4.131.

95 delighting me/ Ralph Hodgson, *Poems* (London, Macmillan, 1918), p. 39.

95 planted a garden/ Bacon, 'Of Gardens', *Essays,* No. 46.

96 the grand Perhaps!/ Browning, *Bishop Blougram's Apology* 182-90, embodying a phrase attributed to the dying Rabelais: *chercher un grand Peut-Estre.*

97 could not answer/ E.g. Matt. xv. 1-9.

97 reason alone/ Matt. xxii. 15-22, John viii. 3-9.

97 by a famous Frenchman/ Ernest Renan, *Prière sur l'Acropole;* a good edition by E. Vinaver and T. B. L. Webster (Manchester [England], 1934).

98 personification of Reason/ Aeschylus, *Prometheus Bound.*

99 immortal souls/ Shakespeare, *The Merchant of Venice,* 5.1.63.

100 INTO MYSTERY/ *Omnia exeunt in mysterium.*

101   'quintessence of dust'/ *Hamlet* 2.2.323f.

102   Byron/ *Journal,* 19 Feb. 1814.

103   unsleeping brain/ On this general topic see H. Poincaré, *Science and Method,* translated by F. Maitland (New York, n.d.), Chap. 3, 'Mathematical Discovery'.

104   current of the soul/ Gray, *Elegy Written in a Country Churchyard* 49-52. 'Noble rage' does not mean anger, but the excited sense of inspiration possessed by genius.

THE MIGRATION OF IDEAS

CHAPTER ONE

Introduction

WHEN we think, there are really only three objects of thought which present themselves to us. We may think about human beings; we may think about the material universe; and we may think about the Divine. All that we teach in schools and universities, all that we ourselves do in the way of continuous and purposeful thinking, is devoted to understanding one of these objects of thought, or else the relation between them.

The scientists have many different ways of thinking about the material universe. Theologians and mystics and poets have been meditating on the Divine for many centuries. All the other arts and disciplines, from music to sociology, are methods of thinking and making statements about human beings.

Now it is difficult even in the sciences to delimit the field of each discipline with hair-line accuracy. It is still more difficult in the humane studies. We all know that the study of a great piece of literature like Dante's *Comedy* or Shakespeare's *Hamlet* will take us into psychology and history—in fact, into several different departments of history—and aesthetics and many other regions where some part of the truth may lie. In a university, we may house the faculties in separate buildings and centre the departments in different offices, but within the realm of thought there are no walls, no soundproof partitions; creative thoughts cannot be divided by as much as the cover of a book.

That is the reason, or one of the reasons, why the humane studies are constantly in flux: expanding and contracting, invading one another's territories, formulating new statements of their purposes and methods, redefining their subject matter. Humanity itself is in constant change, so that only a flexible system of investigation has any chance of finding out important truths about it. We should not deplore or resist this flexibility, but adapt ourselves to it: for man differs from almost all the other inhabitants of this planet in being an enormously adaptable being. Our life, our individual and communal life, is change.

We are going to discuss one of the humane studies, one of the most difficult and the most important. We shall consider its field of interest. We shall ask whether that field might not be extended and redefined in order that more information and more appropriate and important information might be available, and that its investigators might discover new methods of answering problems which have long perplexed them.

This study is history.

History in the broadest sense is the study of the past, and in the most usual sense it is the study of the past activities of human beings. In recent years we have become more and more aware of the importance of history and of its enormous scope; we have been realizing almost involuntarily how much of our lives it includes and how much of our destinies it vitally affects. Our political decisions, our arts and crafts, our industrial and agricultural development, our private lives, our religion are all conditioned by history and are not to be understood without the understanding of history.

We see its importance. But how do we define it? History, we say, is the study of past events. Yes, but of *which* past events? In the second during which we read that question, billions of events took place all over the world; within the flick of an eyelid, another million events occurred; and another, and another million, and another. Now, are all these events the raw material of historical study? Most of them are not even recorded in the newspapers. Some of them will most surely seem to be of trivial importance at this moment, and yet will emerge, in ten or in fifty years, as vital to the lives of thousands of human beings, as genuinely *historic*. How does the historian choose his material? There are always too many facts. They are more multitudinous than the sands of the sea. Sometimes when I see my colleagues in historical research pacing slowly among the shifting and multiplying hills of recorded fact, I think I hear them weep to see such quantities of sand:

> ' If seven maids with seven mops
>   Swept it for half a year,
> Do you suppose,' the Walrus said,
>   ' That they could get it clear? '
> ' I doubt it,' said the Carpenter,
>   And shed a bitter tear.

There, then, is the question we shall consider. *What is history about?* What are the important events, in the past, and in the present which is constantly becoming the past? What are the truly historic phenomena, which are worth recording and analysing? The historian's job is to understand mankind through its past. Now, what are the aspects of the past which will help him to understand mankind most fully?

To begin with, most history is not about individuals but about groups of people. It is about national groups (the Romans, the Chinese, the Spaniards), or social and religious groups (the Quakers, the Virginia planters), or groups of other types (Freemasons, explorers), and it usually discusses individuals only in so far as their activities concern groups. For example, if we set out to learn the history of the American people, we should meet great individuals on the way, but most of our study would be concentrated on the Americans as a group and on their relations with other groups. As well as the story of the physical conquest of the continent, and as well as the description of the changing political and social organization of the citizens of the United States, we should study the records of the detachment of the American colonists from the British empire; American involvement with two other groups, the Red Indians and the African Negroes; the inflow into the existing American group of other groups, Irish and Swedes and Chinese and Italians, and so on; the relations between the United States as a whole and other groups on this continent: Canada, Cuba, Colombia, Argentina; the varying association between the United States and the most powerful political groups in the world: British, Germans, Russians, the peoples of the Far East.

This, I believe, would be generally recognized as the central theme of historical study. The historian investigates the relations between groups of human beings. Now, let us press the question a little further, and ask what kind of relations between groups concern the historian.

The answer most generally given is that the historian studies political relationships, or political and social relationships, viewed principally in terms of *power*. The American Revolution was the successful assertion of the colonists' will to break off a power-link between themselves and Great Britain, and to assume the power to govern themselves. Our relations with the Indians and Negroes have been chiefly those of conqueror and conquered, master and servant. Within our own group much history is stated in terms of the struggle for power—between rival political parties, between capital and labour, business and government, industry and agriculture. There are histories of Europe in which hardly anything seems to happen except dynastic struggles, wars, and revolutions: all shifts of power from one group to another.

Now, is this the whole of history, or most of history? If we select only the facts which illustrate the struggle for power between groups of human beings, and analyse them, shall we have an adequate description of the past? Can we understand our own present condition by viewing it as the outcome of a constant contest for power? Is history the record of conflicts and of wars? Has the human race come so far, and grown so complex and so mighty, *chiefly* by competition and mutual hatred?

As soon as we ask the question, we see that it cannot be answered with a Yes.

In the last half-century we have had two adventures called World Wars (although much of the world's population would think the term an exaggeration). They have been great wars, with much death and destruction. And yet there are more people on the face of the earth now than there have ever been before: their numbers are increasing every minute, every second. The standard of life has not fallen because of these wars. It is rising: plagues and endemic diseases are not spreading; infant mortality is dropping; the area of cultivated land is increasing; roads and transportation routes are multiplying; the world's output of energy is steadily growing; more schools are opening than are being closed; the literacy rate is rising in nearly all countries, and books are pouring off the presses all over the world; new inventions are constantly being made and distributed. Now, all these facts cannot be described as the result of war, or of competition between national groups. There must be some important aspects of the past which cannot be explained in terms of the struggle for political and social power. There must be some other kind of relation between the groups that make up humanity.

Some historians will tell us that the most important explanation is economic rather than political. They will say that history is the record of how one class extracted wealth from another; how alterations in the means of production and distribution changed the social structure of large groups and ultimately of the world; and how different nations exchanged goods and services, thus enriching or exploiting one another. Surely this is true to an important degree. Great chains of events, such as the fall of the Roman Empire or the present decline of Western Europe, cannot be fully understood unless their economic aspects are analysed.

And yet we all know well that the economic explanation of history is inadequate also. In particular, by applying the inappropriate methods of science to human activities involving emotion and will, the economists have given us a partly false picture of the relation between groups. And it is only with the grossest distortion that we can explain such an important occurrence as the rise of Christianity, or the Crusades, or the career and influence of Napoleon, as an economic pattern.

No, there must be some other way of regarding history. There must be some other explanation—not to replace political and social history, not to be substituted for economic history, but rather to complement them, to fill them out and make them real. Probably it ought to be, not a scientific explanation treating men as though they were inanimate objects or forces, but an imaginative explanation, describing fully how men behave as beings of both matter and spirit.

I suggest that we might do well to think of nations, and tribes, and social groups, and even races, not only as political and social rivals, and not only as economic competitors or collaborators, but also as *pupils and teachers*.

I suggest that one of the chief relationships between human groups is, in the broadest sense, *educational*.

I suggest that the history of the world could also be written as a history of the *movement of ideas* from one group of human beings to another. If it were so written, it would both illuminate many areas of the past which are now misunderstood and also—although this is not strictly the duty of the historian—give many of us a much needed confidence in the reason and the future of mankind.

Let us now look at history from this point of view and see whether or not it helps us to comprehend more of the destinies of humanity.

CHAPTER TWO

Politics and Society

IN comparatively recent history there is one remarkable series of events which is best understood as being educational rather than political or economic. A nation of 30,000,000 people deliberately put itself to school, and in a few years learned how to practise innumerable techniques and manage innumerable ideas it had never touched before. This was Japan.

In 1868 the emperor of Japan publicly took an oath, the Charter Oath, to change and reform the empire. This was clearly an announcement of the policy of an important party among his ministers. The final clause of the oath was this:

KNOWLEDGE SHALL BE SOUGHT FOR THROUGHOUT THE WORLD.

From thenceforward it was, and has remained, the permanent policy of the Japanese to learn as much as possible from other nations. This is all the more remarkable because the Japanese are proud people, who dislike putting themselves in a dependent position such as that of pupil to teacher, and they had for many generations distrusted and hated foreigners. But they have a strong will, and once they had determined on this policy they carried it through. Those who determined on it were few in number, but they were surely makers of history.

One of them was Hirobumi Ito. While still a very young man he persuaded his feudal lord, Choshu, to abandon the traditional bows and arrows for rifles and artillery. Soon after that, with his lord's encouragement, he and four others committed a crime for which the penalty was death: they went abroad. They spent a year in London, studying. On their return they became leaders of the progressive party in Japan.[1] In 1882 Ito was commissioned to prepare a Constitution for his country, which until then had had none and had lived in a sort of medieval anarchy with civil wars mitigated by dictatorship. Taking a large staff, Ito went through the countries of Europe, interviewing distinguished people and studying the working of various systems of constitutional government. Seven years later, in 1889, after many discussions and preliminary legislative acts, the new constitution of Japan was promulgated by the emperor. It was modelled on the constitution of Bavaria. The emperor's speech was heard by scores of noblemen and officials. All of them wore European official dress—with one lonely exception, Prince Shimadzu of Satsuma. With his hair dressed in the old style, he appeared in the beautiful medieval

---

[1] In the records of my own college at Oxford University I find the summary of a similar career, which took a Japanese nobleman over the space of six centuries in sixty years. The *Balliol College Register,* 1833-1933, describes the first Japanese member of the college, who came up in 1874:

HACHISUKA, 1st Marquess, Mochi Aki. Born Aug. 1, 1846; son of Prince Nari Hiro Hachisuka; last Feudal Lord of the Tokushima Clan and 16th Daimyo of Japan; Lord of Awaji 1860; Lord of Awa 1868; Governor of the Tokushima prefecture 1869-81, when the Daimyos returned the fief to the emperor; studied in England 1872-9 (aged 28-30 at Balliol); Director of Customs 1880; Minister to France 1882-7; created Marquess 1884; Ambassador to Spain 1885; Commission on Laws 1887; Governor of Tokyo 1890-91; President 1891; Minister of Education 1896; Grand Cordon, Order of the Rising Sun 1903; died 1918.

costume which all Japanese gentlemen had worn for centuries and had now, in less than a single lifetime, dropped. History moves faster through education than through warfare.

Within the same generation other equally revolutionary changes were made in Japan, all by learning from abroad. The old feudal system was abolished, and the old degrees of rank were forgotten: a powerful new hierarchy of princes, marquesses, counts, viscounts, and barons was created on the European model. In 1871 the Chinese calendar, so cumbersome and inaccurate, was abandoned, and the Western calendar officially adopted. Until then Japanese money had been rather like the money of medieval Europe: in 1868 there were four kinds of gold coins, two kinds of silver coins as well as bars and globes of silver, six types of cash, and 1600 different currencies of paper money. This reflected the old division of the country into quasi-independent clan territories. It also allowed the first foreign businessmen who got into Japan to drain away almost all the gold in the country. But in 1872 the Bank of Japan was established, and in a few years the currency was stable. The Bank of Japan was modelled on the Bank of Belgium.

In the same way the Japanese built up their navy and their army. First they sent a mission to Europe to study the organization and training of contemporary defence forces. Then they returned and established the groundwork: central dockyards, arsenals, training schools, a universal draft law, and so on. Then they engaged foreign instructors—a British naval mission for the fleet and a Prussian military mission (headed by General Meckel) for the army. Only a few years later, the navy was efficient enough to destroy the Chinese fleet, and the army of peasants and factory workers overthrew a powerful force of rebellious clansmen in a dangerous civil war. The subsequent history of the Japanese army and navy we know.

The Japanese did not merely go abroad to learn. Under the Charter Oath they brought in no less than 5000 men and women teachers from abroad, including 1200 Americans. (They were first called *yatoi,* 'hired aliens', and later, when they justified themselves, *o yatoi,* 'honourable hired aliens'.) W. E. Griffis, who was one of them, recalled how strange it was to teach young men who were longing for knowledge, and who eagerly received all the instruction he could give them, and then to walk home along streets that were still in the Middle Ages, passing (it might well be) the corpse of a poor man on whom a samurai had tested a new backswing of his powerful sword. In a panegyric on his colleagues, Griffis cries:

> Noble are the records of Pumpelly in mining, of Brunton in lighthouse-engineering . . . of Knipping in meteorology . . . of Milne in initiating the science of seismology, of Lyman in revealing true geology, of Baeltz and Scriba in anatomy, physiology, and ethnology.

Of course, it would be a misrepresentation to suggest that all this learning came to Japan with lightning rapidity and utterly without preparation. As early as 1741 the Shogun Yoshimune had ordered two scholars to learn Dutch (the Dutch being then the only Europeans allowed to visit Japan); and in 1771 a Japanese physician, Sugita, got hold of a German-Dutch manual of anatomy, tested its truth by watching a dead body being dissected, and then had it translated and published. Western painting, geography, and astronomy were beginning to be studied about the same time. But all this was, proportionately, only preparation for the great educational revolution of the 1860s and succeeding decades.

The whole story is astonishing. It is even more astonishing to realize that it happened not once in the history of Japan but twice. Far back in the Dark Ages, the Japanese had apparently been a Mongolian tribe which (like the 'Indians' of America) drifted eastward in search of a home. They found it in the islands, which they conquered and cultivated. As they grew in numbers and security, they determined to become civilized. They were on the fringe of the highly civilized Chinese empire; and in A.D. 645 they adopted much of its civilization without becoming its vassals. From China they learned, and introduced into their own society, a centralized bureaucracy; Buddhism as a higher religion; writing, based on Chinese script; the principles of fine art, which are really Chinese art simplified; and many other appurtenances of civilization.

And now it has happened a third time. The United States, after defeating Japan militarily and truncating its power economically occupied the country for a number of years. And which was the most important act, the one which will have most powerful effects in the future? Military conquest, or economic mastery? Or will it prove to have been the process of education that took place during those years?

There, then, is one example of the movement of ideas from one group to another, and of the enormous historical effects which this movement can have. Of course this way of looking at history raises special problems of its own. For instance, we should like to know how the transference of ideas into the minds of the Japanese was made; why it was initiated, what motives drove men like Ito and Sugita; who were the leaders in the movement, and what was their relation to the rest of the country. We should also like to understand the differentiae: for instance, why did the learning process work out so differently in Japan and in its neighbouring country, China? We must think over these questions as we go on.

There are many more examples of this movement of ideas as an important historical force. The story of Turkey is another.

When the Turks entered modern history in the Middle Ages, they were a small group of nomads moving westward out of central Asia. Full of vigour and energy, they drove in upon the eastern Roman empire, attacked it doggedly for generations, and ultimately took it over. Like the Japanese, they remained a medieval nation until almost within living memory, and they have retained some medieval traits today. But after the Ottoman empire was lost in 1918, the Turks—or rather the governing group of the Turks—determined to learn from European nations and to convert Turkey into a modern, Westernized people. Within ten short years, between 1925 and 1934, our own Roman letters were introduced (no books were printed in Arabic script after 1928); universities and schools were reorganized and enlarged; the metric system of measurement was introduced; polygamy was abolished, and women were given the vote; a new civil code of law was adopted, modelled on Swiss law; English (rather than Arabic, Persian, or French) was made the second language; the old titles, such as pasha, were dropped, the fez of the Middle East was abolished and the hat substituted (similarly the wearing of European dress is official in Japan for nearly all important functions).

The enormous results of these two enterprises, in Japan and Turkey, can be measured by comparing these nations with other potentially powerful groups in the Middle and Far East. Suppose that the densely populated land of Java, or the rich land of Burma, had been educated in the same way as the Japanese educated themselves; or suppose that the swarming millions of Egyptians had determined to learn from the West in the same way as the Turks: who can doubt that the history of the world would have been radically different—especially in the last thirty and the coming seventy years?

From an earlier period there is a similar but even more important case of history being made by education. This is the process which began in ancient Rome about 250 B.C.

Like the Turks and the Japanese, the Romans first appear in history as a simple people, brave, conservative, uneducated, peripheral, and rather unpromising. They were peasants clustered about a few little towns in a fertile plain, mixed (if the legends are true) with outlaws and masterless men, and dominated for a time by the brilliant and sinister Etruscans, a far more highly civilized race; one might have expected them to remain rooted in their fields for many centuries while history swept over their heads like the changing seasons. But some obscure and almost unanalysable drive propelled them outward: they grew and grew, they learned and adapted, until they became the conquerors and defenders of the civilized world. Now, the Romans had many merits which fitted them to be governors. They believed in law, not in arbitrary will. They believed in self-discipline rather than self-expression. They drew no colour line. They were fine technologists—road-builders and engineers and town planners: it was really the Romans, with their enormous irrigation systems, who transformed the western Mediterranean land region from jungles and deserts into a rich country of orchards and vineyards and prosperous fields, keeping it so for five hundred years. Even if they had done no more than abolish savagery, organize production and commerce, and establish a world-wide rule of law, they would have been well remembered; but they would have been remembered as the makers of a material civilization.

The Romans knew, however, that civilization was much more than material wealth. They determined to introduce meaning into their culture, to give themselves more than what they could eat and drink and play with. In the second century they conquered Greece; and almost at once (as a Roman poet puts it) they became its prisoners.

To express this in our own terms, the Romans became the willing pupils of Greece. Like the Japanese in the nineteenth century, they brought in tutors from abroad: Greek experts to lecture to them, Greek scientists to improve their knowledge and practice of the sciences, Greek philosophers to live with them. Many of the greatest Romans had Greek thinkers living permanently in their homes, in order to keep up their intellectual standards by constant discussion of lofty and difficult subjects. For instance, the younger Cato, the republican opponent of Caesar, the man whom we think of as a stern traditional Roman, was in fact a thinker trained by the Stoic philosopher Athenodorus Cordylio, who lived in his home. Roman homes were decorated by Greek artists. Their literature was formed on Greek models, with the exception of a very few literary types, such as satire; and the proudest boast of a Roman author was that he had, in his own language, equalled one of the Greek masters.

The result of this was not, as we might expect, to create

a culture that was a mere copy of Greece. By tradition, by social structure, by education, the Romans differed profoundly from the Greeks. They knew that they were relatively stupid, so they learned from Greece; they felt that they were insensitive to art, so they got Greek artists to make their lives beautiful; but they were not ashamed of their own qualities—moral sense, patriotism, responsibility, and a consciousness of time that the eternally youthful Greeks never possessed. They knew their language was less flexible and more limited in range than Greek; but they were not ashamed of its power and energy and its sombre music. Therefore they wrote poems, plays, speeches, philosophical dialogues, and histories which no Greek could have composed, and yet which were clearly modelled on Greek types.

In fact, the Romans contributed to a civilization that had two phases, two complementary aspects, harmonizing like treble and bass in a great instrument. The Greeks produced philosophers; the Romans produced statesmen, who had learned from the Greeks to be philosophers, too, and therefore greater statesmen. The Greeks developed oratory; the Romans put ethical and social content into it. The Greeks worked out exquisite lyric metres and filled them with delicate feeling. The Romans took over the form, deepened the feeling, and added profounder thought. Before the rise of Rome it is possible to talk of Greek culture; but from 250 B.C. or so it is really better to speak of the Greco-Roman civilization, to which both belonged, in which one had been master and the other pupil, and in which finally both were friendly rivals and challenging collaborators.

The Roman Empire. The very phrase sounds as though we were writing history exclusively in military and political terms, to which an economic explanation might be added.

But such descriptions are inadequate. It would be more revealing to consider the whole complex as an educational process. Of course it can be portrayed as a series of bloody conquests and vain rebellions, with the eagles of the legions turned to vultures above the bleeding bodies of myriads of unhappy tribesmen; and it can certainly be described as a tremendous racket, in which economic exploitation and waste ran wild and wrecked a whole society. But there was something else in it, and that something else was the aspect of more permanent value: its will and its ability to educate. It is for their educational value that we still study the classics of Greece and Rome; and it is for their power to educate that we admire the Romans. We are their pupils.

For it was Rome who civilized and taught the barbarians who were the ancestors of most of us: the Spaniards, the Gauls, the British, the Balkan peoples, the Rumanians, and the North Africans. Rome found them scattered tribes living in the early Iron Age, illiterate and poor. In a few generations she taught them agriculture, trade, architecture, and industry; in a few more she taught them law, philosophy, literature, and religion. Perhaps these people could scarcely have assimilated Greek civilization directly, even if they had had the opportunity: it was too intense, too difficult, too highly developed. But as passed through the coarser mind of Rome, it became comprehensible and acceptable to the recently civilized savages. And Rome added much that was her own: notably the sense of law; and, I think, an un-Greek seriousness about religion.

And finally, the greatest lesson taught to our ancestors through Rome was Christianity. Like so much else in that civilization it began in the Middle East, and in its early days was Greek-speaking; then it was translated into Latin

10

and transformed into something Roman. Both the Greek and the Roman elements can be traced in Christianity, as well, of course, as the original Hebrew foundation; but I confess that most of *our* Christianity reminds me of Rome. When I see a Spanish monk in a painting by Zurbaran or study the face of one of the New England Puritans or Scots Covenanters, I seem to myself to be looking at one of the Romans whom we see in portrait-statues or carved upon altars, gravely sacrificing, with deep lines in their faces and with their heads covered in reverence. These are our ancestors.

We have looked at three cases in which history was made by education: Japan; Turkey; and the civilization of Greece and Rome, which flowed into our ancestors' minds, which indeed is still educating us. Surely it is scarcely possible to understand any nation, or any group, through its *own* history alone; surely we must always inquire, 'Who were its most powerful teachers and what did it learn from them?' Take one further example, the proud and fiercely nationalist Spaniards. How can we understand their character without thinking of those who helped to make it? The moment you enter a great Spanish city you will see and hear two things which scarcely exist elsewhere in Europe. One is the bull ring, which is the only existing descendant of the Roman amphitheatre with its systematized killing. The other is flamenco singing, which is, perhaps, ultimately Arabian in origin. And if we go back into comparatively recent history, we shall learn more about the Spaniards by seeing them as pupils.

In A.D. 711 the Arabs crossed the straits of Gibraltar. Seven years later they had conquered almost the entire peninsula of Spain and were crossing the Pyrenees. Except for a tiny remnant in the northwest, the entire population was subjugated. The Spaniards had been Romans, sharing in that culture; but since the fall of the Western empire and the conquest of Spain by incoming barbarians, their culture had declined. The Arabs were rather more civilized at this time, and certainly their civilization was more cohesive. They loved music and poetry, fine clothes and fine architecture, gardens and beautiful furniture, philosophy and delicate sensibilities. Within a few generations, much of Spain had become Mohammedan; and even those who remained Christians sometimes adopted Arab dress, admired the Arab aesthetics and ways of life, and strove to write in the fine Arabian hand.

Now, there are many consequences of this, too complex to analyse now. But one of the oddest is that the Arabs helped to create modern European lyric poetry. No less than five languages were used in Spain under the Arabs, and doubtless many more dialects. What we know as Spanish was too vague in shape, and too newly born, and too unlearned to be considered fit for literature. Yet it was—as it is now—vigorous. The people sang songs to it, and fitted it to dance rhythms, and talked it. Their poems and songs were hardly ever written down: hardly considered worth writing. They had, apparently, to be stylized before they became literature—they were its raw material.

About A.D. 900 an Arab poet called Mucaddam invented a new kind of lyric called the *muwashshaha,* which 'broke the forms of the classical Arabic metre and violated its purity of style' by bringing in verses in vulgar Arabic and spoken Spanish. He was in fact taking over folk song and stylizing it into literature. Some Hebrew poems similar to his work have been found dating to A.D. 1100 or thereabouts, and containing primitive Spanish verses—quatrains with the second and fourth lines echoing by assonance, a form that was once believed to have been unknown before the sixteenth century.

But apart from this it has been suggested that the first lyric poetry of southern Europe, which begins so suddenly about 1100 in Provence with a short collection of poems by the Count of Poitiers, Guillaume IX, was really based on Arab poems, both in style and in subject matter, and took from them the rhyme scheme AAAB; the five-line and seven-line strophe form; the refrain; fictitious names for girls, like Bel Esper; the spring atmosphere; commonplaces about the torments of love (weeping, insomnia, cruelty of the beloved, internal fires); the idea that the lover is the slave of the beloved. It has also been pointed out that the connection of love and philosophy, love and non-religious quasi-mystical idealism, was re-entering the Western world through the Arabs. A famous work on the subject is the *Tawq*, by Ibn Hazm, written in 1022, which mentions Plato and stresses the spiritual, the uplifting, aspects of love.

Any detailed study of the meeting of cultures and the migration of ideas would certainly consider the angle of convergence. It would ask whether the two cultures that met had much in common, or little; and if they had little in common, it would doubtless point to much discord and misery caused by that meeting. It is surely the width of this angle of divergence which accounts for the unhappiness of Negroes in a predominantly white society. But the question can be studied in a less ticklish context: the association between the Spaniards and the Indians. In North America white men and Indians have not blended. Sometimes the Indians have been assimilated; sometimes they have been isolated on reservations; they have seldom mingled with white people to produce something new and harmonious. But the blend has occurred in Spanish America, although it is not yet complete.

Consider. The Spaniards had many traits in their culture which (by coincidence) the Indians also had; and they had others that altered the Indians' culture without utterly destroying it, such as these: courage, contempt for death, fascination by death; reticence, broken by wild rhetoric and boasting; deep sense of religion; a taste for cruelty often purified by Christianity in the Spaniards (but remember the Penitentes); harsh realism, balanced by lofty mysticism.

In other things the two nations differ profoundly. But there was a basis of spiritual agreement between them. The result was that, just as Rome penetrated into Spain and changed it into a new thing, so Spain penetrated into Indian America and changed it into a new thing. Perhaps its transformation is not yet complete, but it is in process; and it is not irrelevant to notice that two of the best poems dealing with the Indians have been written in Spanish (Ercilla's *Araucana* and Hernández' *Martin Fierro*) and to point to the music of the Mexican Carlos Chavez as full of deep understanding of both cultures.

Let us look back and see how far we have come in this discussion.

We began by saying that history was the study of human beings through the analysis of their past. Then we asked which aspects of the past were worth studying, and we agreed that history was chiefly about the relations between groups of people.

From there we went on to ask how these relations should be described. Most history books treat them in terms of power; and yet competition will not explain all or much of the destinies of humanity. Others treat them as economic relationships, but that is also an inadequate view of our past.

We then suggested that one of the most important relationships between groups was educational, and that much history could be viewed in terms of the movement of ideas from one group to another.

In looking for examples of this, the first we found was the rise of Japan through learning and assimilating foreign ideas; and we saw that Japan had made this important step three times—once in the Dark Ages of the seventh century, once in the nineteenth century, and now again under American tutelage in the twentieth.

Another example was Turkey. A third was ancient Rome, which made itself a pupil of Greece; and we saw how Rome had passed its knowledge on to the barbarians.

Finally we glanced at the peculiar educational association of the Arabs with Spain; and of the Spaniards with the American Indians.

No doubt many other examples of the movement of ideas between national and racial groups could be found in the realm of society and politics; but these will suffice at present. Meanwhile, it is stimulating to look over human history from this point of view. There are many different kinds of maps. Some of them show simply the countries and races of the world, coloured and motionless, lying there as though there were no communication between them, separated by sharp frontiers. Others show the drift of ocean currents, the rush of winds, the tides of weather which pass constantly back and forth above and beside the countries of the earth; and these remind us, much more than the political maps, that we live in a planetary unit. To consider the movement of thought throughout the world is, in a way, like making a new map, in which we can see distant countries connected by invisible tides, intellectual currents moving by strange paths around the whole globe and uniting the manifold minds of men into something like a single, mighty, super-human Reason. It is as though the earth were thinking.

POLITICS AND SOCIETY : BIBLIOGRAPHY

W. E. Griffis, *The Japanese Nation in Evolution,* New York, 1907.

J. H. Gubbins, *The Making of Modern Japan,* London, 1920.

D. Keene, *The Japanese Discovery of Europe,* London, 1952.

R. Menéndez-Pidal, 'The Origins of Romance Literature in the Light of a Recent Discovery', *Measure* 2 (1951), 428-41.

A. R. Nykl, *Hispano-Arabic Poetry and Its Relations with the Old French Troubadours,* Baltimore, 1936.

CHAPTER THREE

Religion and Art

RELIGION is one of the prime sources of artistic feeling and creation; and art is one of the chief expressions of religious thought. Throughout the world, from the pagodas of China to the sculptures of Mexico, much of the most powerful and sensitive artistic work created by men has been created in homage and service to the gods. And indeed, it is not possible to understand any religion in its strength and weakness without appreciating the art it has evoked among its worshippers. The strong simple hymns and sermons of the Protestant Church, the grandiose baroque altars of the Roman Catholics, the vast and sombre mosaic portraits of the Greek Orthodox Church—these express three different and, I dare say, three equally valid approaches to Christianity.

Yet there are some religions that are inadequately expressed in art: either because the craftsmen failed to develop technical skill, or because of some spiritual deficiency, some rejection or apparently insoluble contradiction, within the minds of the worshippers. And sometimes a religion has failed to find artistic expression for a long time, only to achieve it at a comparatively late stage under the influence of some new idea or stimulus from without. One of the most striking examples of this fact, and one which brilliantly illustrates the migration of ideas, is the art of Buddhism. There is now a huge quantity of Buddhistic art; statues, friezes, paintings, temples, and minor decorations embodying the life and teachings of Buddha throng the Far East, and every visitor to a Western museum has seen at least one sculptured portrait of Buddha himself—the calm figure with the gently draped robes, every line of his face and body expressing peace. But during the first five centuries of Buddhism there was little or no such Buddhistic art. Its appearance was a novelty, caused by the importation of Greek ideas.

Buddhism—like Christianity and Mohammedanism—is a higher religion created in a climate of polytheism; like them, it teaches peace and charity, and certainty, and eternal justice. Buddha himself was a prince of northern India, who lived from 563 to 483 B.C. (His name was Siddattha Gautama, and he was the heir of the Sakyas, northeast of Oudh. Buddha is his title, and means Enlightened.) When he was quite a young man, he left his home, deserting his wife and son and renouncing his right and duty to succeed his father, in order to find some way of rising above the constant flux of human desires and destinies. For years he practised the fearful austerities of the Indian mystics, but then renounced them as useless. He passed through a long period of loneliness, doubt, and temptation; but at last, after tremendous efforts of his intellect and his whole soul, he attained Enlightenment. He worked out a new gospel, a new way of life covering both ethics and religion and aimed at securing perfect peace of soul. This he taught for many years, wandering up and down northern India with a group of pupils; and then, when very old, he died as peacefully as he had lived.

After his death, the traditions of his life and works began to grow into a large gospel, elaborated with Oriental imagination; relics of his earthly existence were treasured, shrines, hermitages, and monasteries sprang up, decorated with memories of the Enlightened One. But for several hundreds of years, no Indian artist ventured to portray Buddha himself. Why? It is very hard to say. Foucher, who knew more about Oriental art and thought than almost any other critic in the field, suggested that it was simply 'not the custom'; but that is a little like begging the question, and perhaps the true solution lies in the fact that Buddha was almost impossible to portray. He was more than a man; but he was not a god. He taught meditation, and abstinence, and peace; but these teachings are hard to translate into painting and sculpture. In any case, it is certain that for at least five hundred years after Buddha died, his face and body were never shown in Buddhist art. This is strange. But it is even more strange that the Indian artists often depicted scenes from his life and teaching, crowded with other figures, and deliberately omitted Buddha even when he must have been the central figure.

For instance, at Sanchi there is a sculptured frieze showing the dramatic scene in which the young prince rode away from his house forever. There is his horse. There are the deities who attended him and assisted his escape. But there is no Buddha. The saddle is empty. In this and in all other early Buddhistic scenes, no part of the master's bodily form is shown. At most, we see his footprints ('a direct ideographic transcription of the formula used in India to designate a person viewed with respect'); or the umbrella, which is a sign of his rank as prince; or an empty throne to which one of the devout is paying homage; or the Wheel of the Law, to symbolize his teaching. Nothing more.

And then, in one corner of the Buddhist world, suddenly, unexpectedly, without development or native forerunners,

RELIGION AND ART 145

there appears a large and impressive collection of sculpture grouped around vivid and often handsome portraits of the Buddha. Instead of an empty throne, we see a human figure, noble and thoughtful. Instead of an empty saddle, we see a young prince riding on his horse. Alone, or surrounded by his disciples, the type of Buddha has at last been established.

Now, where did this sudden advance take place, and who initiated it?

All these sculptures come from a land which was once devoted to Buddhism, but which is now Moslem: a land which seems, during the intervening centuries, to have become less fertile and populous, and which has certainly changed its language and probably its racial character. It is called (for the purpose of this study) Gandhâra. It lies in the extreme northwest of Pakistan, and borders on Afghanistan and Kashmir: a land of rolling dusty hills and rocky valleys, lying between Peshawar and Lahore. (The name itself may be perpetuated in Kandahar.) More than a century after Buddha's death, this land was reached by Alexander the Great; and about the second century B.C. it was invaded and conquered by Greek princes working their way up from the Middle East. They set up a kingdom, a sort of crossroads kingdom, in which Greek civilization met and mingled with the culture of the great central Asiatic plains and also with the civilization of India itself. And apparently even after the original Greek princes had been superseded, the Gandhâra kingdom continued to communicate with the world of Greek imagination and thought through the lands of the Middle East.

It was in this place, and under the impulse of Greek concepts of art and religion, that the first sculptured representations of Buddha were made. From there they spread all over the rest of the Orient. The date of this is still disputed, but the best-informed opinion points to the second century of the Christian era—a period when Greek aesthetic ideals were spreading through the Roman Empire as far as Britain and Rumania and north Germany, and were travelling all through the Middle East: that was a happy and a prosperous century. The names of artists who initiated this revolutionary change are of course unknown; but we know roughly who they were: they must have been Greeks, or people of Greek sympathies with Greek training, who had become interested in Buddhism.[1] The problem of portraying the Enlightened One as a being both human and superhuman was put to them; and, because they thought as Greeks, they were able to solve it. Greek religion was unlike most other ancient religions in that it was almost wholly anthropomorphic. The Egyptians worshipped gods with animal heads; other ancient peoples adored the sun and the planets or, like the Romans, personifications whom they could not picture; but the gods of the Greeks were human in form though superhuman in power and in beauty.

Therefore, the first statues of Buddha show him unmistakably not as an Oriental sage, but as the god Apollo. His hair is not cut off or his head shaven as it should have been: it is richly wavy, gathered in a knot just like the hair of the Apollo Belvedere. His robe falls around him in graceful folds, as in the Greek portrait-statues. His expression—ah, his expression is the most revealing of all: for in those early statues he is shown with his eyes open and his lips almost curved as though about to break into a smile, with the

---

[1] Super suggests that Antoninus Pius sent a master-sculptor out to Peshawar after receiving a mission from 'the Indians' (see Aurelius Victor 15).

serene, gracious expression of Apollo, the god of male
beauty, of healing, of light, and of divination. The only
trace of Buddha's Oriental character in such a statue is that
the lobes of his ears are pierced and lengthened, to show
that he has taken out and discarded the rings that were part
of his princely jewellery. Sometimes he has a halo, or nimbus, behind his head—a feature not found in purely Indian
Buddhist sculpture, and indeed far more closely connected
with the light-deity Apollo.

But there are other portrayals of Buddha which are not
modelled on a Greek god. Sometimes he appears as a
thoughtful young man, standing. He wears a long robe
skilfully gathered around him and draped so as to expose
his right arm and shoulder: the arm is bent as though it
were at any moment to be used as a meaningful gesture.
Here we see at a glance that Buddha has been modelled on
another Greek type: the type of the intellectual—teacher,
orator, or philosopher, best known from the statue of Sophocles in the Lateran Museum and the famous portrait of
Demosthenes.

Besides these individual portraits, there are many Gandhâra sculptures that show Buddha accompanied by human
beings and deities. One of these is a procession: it is the
renunciation scene, in which the earlier artists had portrayed
merely the horse with an empty saddle. But the Gandhâra
sculptors put Buddha on horseback, and surround him with
deities in an orderly group—the deities with the heavenly
half-smile of Greek gods on their lips. And as we look at it,
we see that this scene is inspired by another type of Western
art, Greco-Roman this time. In composition, in poses, in
style generally, it is modelled on those reliefs that show the
triumphal arrival or departure of a Roman emperor, enter-

ing or leaving a city. And the strange thing is that there is in existence a Christian sarcophagus, or stone coffin, from the fourth century, which shows a very similar procession on its sides: but here the subject is Christ riding into Jerusalem on Palm Sunday, another triumphal progress. In other episodes of the life of Buddha, we can see how the sculptors were inspired to model their portraits on scenes from the lives of the Roman emperors, executed with Greek taste and technique. Once Buddha converted a murderer, Angulimalya, who threw himself on his knees and bowed his head to the ground before the master: as we look at the scene, we recall the barbarian prostrating himself before the Roman conqueror, on the Arch of Constantine.[1]

One or two of these resemblances might be coincidence; but the entire assemblage is absolutely convincing. And critics point out other debts the Indian sculptors owe to their Greek colleagues. It was from them that the Indians learned how to introduce symmetry into their reliefs. It was from them that they learned how to use blank space to give a feeling of room and distance in their carvings. In fact, it was from them that the Indians learned how to treat stone as stone: for their earlier carving had really resembled painting transferred to stone, but now they acquired that feeling for solidity and volume and air and light which is the quality of Greek sculpture.

Many figures and sculptural elements found in the Gandhâra district look almost wholly Greek, and scarcely Oriental at all. There are pillars that end in acanthus leaves, in a

[1] A contemporary expert has measured some of the standing Buddhas and finds that nearly all of them are carved in the peculiar proportion of five heads to the total height—the proportion of the sculptures of the period of Constantine at Rome: its purpose is to concentrate attention on the *head* rather than on the body.

style which has been called Indo-Corinthian; sometimes little figures appear among the leaves as they do in the capitals of the Baths of Caracalla at Rome. There are carven friezes in which children, or youthful deities, are shown carrying a long undulating garland beneath one of the scenes of Buddha's life; and other such children appear holding a halo above his head. Perhaps they have some divine name in India; but we recognize them as Cupids. There is a relief that shows two armed men, a terrified woman, and a horse on wheels moving toward a city wall; it is not hard to recognize Troy, and the Wooden Horse, and Sinon and Laocoön, although the voluptuous female figure, with the slender waist and swelling hips, looks more like an Indian princess than like Cassandra. There are Bacchanalian processions, with the Maenads dancing to the clash of their cymbals and the drunken god Silenus riding slowly along among them—these remind us that according to legend the god Dionysus himself invaded India and taught the Indians the use of the vine. Strange it is, so far from the sea, to find a frieze of powerful sea gods carrying oars and dolphins; and stranger still to find sea monsters, both human and animal: the winged horses with dragon tails who represent the power of the waves and the Tritons or ichthyocentaurs, bearded, hooved, and dragon-tailed, who, in the Mediterranean, would have been blowing their wreathed horns, but who, transported to the land of religious mysticism, kneel beside Buddha clasping their hands in the typical Indian gesture of reverence. Once we have accepted—as any dispassionate observer must do—the Greek influence in the Gandhâra sculptures, we can trace it again and again: a murderer, leaning on his club, reminds us of Hercules; a spirit of the air, with a huge naked torso and an unruly beard, recalls both Hercules and Atlas; a Bodhisattva, one of Buddha's earlier incarnations, is a gentle youth with downbent head and bearing garlands, in whom we recognize Antinous.

It was from this centre, then, that the sculptured portrayal of Buddha was taught to the whole of the Buddhist world. Naturally he changed as he was depicted by artists in different lands: Ceylon, Java, Indo-China, Japan, southern India, China, Tibet. It is instructive to watch the changes that affected him in later Indian art. The sculptors never dared to abolish the hair with which his first Greek portraitists had endowed him; but they stylized it and reduced it to curls clinging to his head; they made his drapery thinner, as though changing it from the Greek wool into the Oriental cotton, and made it almost part of the body, thus losing the beautiful effect produced in Greek sculpture by the differing treatment of cloth and of the body beneath the cloth; they made his body bigger, they set him on a giant lotus flower; they converted him into something much more like a gigantic idol; and, most significant of all, they made the eyes—which had once looked calmly out of the beautiful Apollonian face to survey the external world—gradually close into slits of meditation, withdrawn and passionless. But in spite of all these changes, the iconographical formulas that were worked out by the early Gandhâra sculptors are preserved hundreds of years later and thousands of miles away; and it is possible, even in the face of a Chinese Buddha, to detect something of the charm of a Greek deity, to remember something Greek in the fall of his robe, and, strangest of all, to see in the 'hill of knowledge' on top of his head a reminiscence of the richly knotted hair of the young Apollo.

There, then, is one powerful and convincing instance of the transmission of ideas in the field of religion and art. It was the Greeks who made the Indians able to see the bodily form of their own saviour. Thereby they assisted the development of Buddhism from a philosophy ('hinayana') into a religion ('mahayana') and provided a powerful vehicle to propagandize it throughout the Far Eastern world.

Turn away from the East now; turn westward; and we shall find that it was the Greeks who made it possible for us to depict, in art, our Saviour and the incidents of his life and legend. Not long ago a German expedition to Central Asia discovered a little sculptured group in the Gandhâra area. It showed a powerful adult male, with his legs bare to the mid-thigh, carrying a little child-figure on one shoulder. It was identified easily enough from Indian literature as the god of wealth, Pancika; and that is how it seemed to those who adored it in India. But if we look at it with Christian eyes, we see it as another group of holy figures. We see it as St. Christopher carrying the Infant Jesus across the river on his shoulder—the scene that appears on so many St. Christopher medals. If now we can make a further effort of imagination and look at it with the eyes of a pagan or an art historian (sometimes almost the same thing) we shall see it as it originally was: Hermes, or Hercules, carrying the infant Dionysus. The same theme, the same grouping, the same idea, spread both eastward and westward and was adopted into two different religions because of its beauty and its power.

Although this perhaps does not come within our plan, yet it is so striking and so interesting that it deserves mention. The early Christians had no description of the appearance of Jesus; and apart from the tradition of the miraculous

11

portrait of Veronica, they had no drawing or painting of him. And yet they wondered what he looked like. Some of them doubted whether it would be right to make pictures of Jesus. (The same doubt, ultimately based on the Second Commandment against the making of images, led to the terrible civil strife in which the Iconoclasts almost broke up the empire of Byzantium.) We do not know what prompted their decision to try to portray Jesus and the Christian story, but it may well have been the diminishing influence of Judaism and the increasing power of Greek ideals in the early Church. (This same movement can be traced in the rise of Christian hymnology, the development of Christian oratory, and the elaboration of Christian philosophy. It is equally marked in the development of Christian ritual, through which the communion table was turned into an altar, one of the faithful into a priest, and the communion meal itself into a 'mystery' in which not all took equal part—and which in some churches occurs behind a veil, curtain, or gate, thus replacing the very idea of brotherly communion by an earlier mystery notion.) Hence it is that the first sculptures and paintings that have come down to us from early Christianity are pagan in plan and execution.

The most obvious example is that of the Christian angel. We know the type: a being with flowing hair, long floating robes, and large wings. On the whole it looks more feminine than masculine. In the Gospels the angels are not described: their name means simply 'messenger'; and their sex is masculine. Whence the change? and whence the detail? It comes from pagan Greek poetry and sculpture, for the angel as now known to us is simply the Winged Victory.

Saints and divine persons in Christian art nearly always wear a ring of brightness around their heads. This is not described in the Bible, where at moments of glorification the entire figure is surrounded and perhaps invaded by light. It has been taken over from the nimbus of pagan sculpture, and we have already seen how it also travelled east to settle on the head of Buddha.

The figure of Jesus himself could hardly be conceived by a Greco-Roman Christian sculptor as a Jewish rabbi. So the artists sought for classical, pagan types, and found them. There are several statuettes of Jesus as the Good Shepherd, with a lamb across his shoulders: they are adapted from the earlier portrayals of the god Hermes with a lamb across his shoulders, Hermes the patron of flocks and herds. But Jesus was also the Logos, the voice of Reason, the inimitable teacher; and so he was depicted in the robe and with the gesture and pose of a Greek teacher. Yet neither of these poses fully showed his miraculous power; and therefore in the Catacombs he was shown seated, and surrounded by charmed animals, in the manner of Orpheus, musician, poet, miracle-worker, raiser from the dead, and founder of a mystical religion.

In this way the long process of interpenetration of pagan and Christian art began. It was to continue for many centuries: over a thousand years later, when the Laocoön was discovered, Titian was to adapt the pose of one of the dying Trojan boys for his painting of St. Sebastian, and El Greco was to use, and characteristically to distort, the poses of all three figures for a memorable picture of the Resurrection of Our Lord. Art without tradition is like a plant without rich, deep soil.

This world has seen many wonderful teachers, but among the most wonderful are surely the missionaries of various religions. And the most wonderful educative processes are those which have taken place after the introduction of a strange and distant religion into a national group which felt completely alien to it, and yet could use and assimilate it. A book could be written on missionaries—not only the missionaries of Christianity, but also the missionaries of all higher religions and of philosophies, too, such as Stoicism. They are an inspiring set of men, saints and heroes.

In the transmission of ideas, the missionaries of the world's religions have not all been equally effective. A thorough study of missionary activity would reveal certain general principles, but at present we may say tentatively that an effective missionary carries more than his religion; is not alone but part of a group, collective or serial; welcomes assimilation to the society in which he is a missionary but maintains some sort of dominance, intellectual or social; derives continuous inspiration from a mother society; thrives on competition, but perishes when it becomes too intense. For example, Roman Catholic missionaries to the Pueblo-Indians do not produce much effect when they are Irish-American by origin; and yet there are records of Christian Iroquois converting whole groups of Indians to whom they were strangers, merely by contact—because that contact was more complete.

We might describe the work of the Nestorian ('Assyrian') missionaries, who made such amazing journeys all over the Far East from their home in Assyria during the period between the fall of the Roman Empire and the Renaissance (at one time they were the sole Christian Church in Asia, and twice they bid fair to convert the Chinese), but who failed—probably because of the constant attacks on their mother church and the difficulty of communication. But for sheer effectiveness in the transmission of ideas we must single out the Buddhist and Jesuit missionaries. Both of these small groups changed the world: every one of their members produced effects a thousandfold greater than the average man.

Buddhism began as a small philosophical creed, limited to northern India, with no written doctrine, no organized church, and in fact a quietist attitude which might well have prevented it from spreading. There have been many such creeds all over the world. It was apparently the conversion of King Asoka (*c.* 240 B.C.) which started its expansion into a world religion—a position it still holds even although it has shrunk in its homeland.

Ceylon is said to have been converted by Asoka's son Mahinda; it is still the site of a mighty Buddhist shrine.

China was never converted; but Buddhism entered it and Buddhism is still there. In A.D. 62 (says the tradition) the Han emperor Ming-Ti dreamed of a Golden Man, and sent an embassy westward to discover who he was. The embassy brought back two monks, who began to teach not only Buddhism but astronomy and apparently the decimal system of numerology. From then on, Chinese pilgrims kept going to India, bringing back Indian books and translating them: such was Hsüan-Ch'uang, who brought home a library of Sanskrit volumes and spent the last nineteen years of his life putting them into Chinese.

Japan was reached through Korea in the sixth century of the Christian era. The first Buddhist missionary is said to have been a monk from China called Shiba Tachito, who landed, built a temple, and continued to worship Buddha for many years alone, until other missions brought in a fuller knowledge of Buddhism and helped it to find acceptance.

The effects of Buddhism in other countries are both easy and difficult to assess. Obviously Buddhism produced a tremendous amount of architecture, both good and bad; and a profound alteration in society by diverting thousands of men and women from secular life into monasteries and nunneries.

Further, the historians point to changes in the art and the poetry of China and Japan effected by Buddhism. For instance, they assert that block printing was invented in order to multiply the sacred texts. They say with great assurance that Buddhism produced a new and (from the world's point of view) an extremely valuable style of painting: the mystical, deliberately inadequate, imaginative style known to both China and Japan. In Japan it is called *Sumiye*: it is black and white, in ink, done on the thinnest paper possible, and its aim is to be rapid and spontaneous and incomplete, because life is all those things. We are told also that it was Zen Buddhism which inspired the invention, or rather the revitalization, of the Japanese 17-syllable poetic form, the *haiku,* by Basho. Before him it had been only a method of word-play, an epigram; but he made it a little window on the universe.[1] Experts also relate to Zen

---

[1] E.g. ' The cry of the grasshopper gives no sign that it is soon to die' (Basho).

'Blessed is the beggar, who wears heaven and earth for summer clothes' (Kikaku).

'I enjoyed the cool evening with one who does not say all he thinks' (Hyakuchi).

'In this crystal spring the stones at the bottom seem to move' (Soseki).

'"Oh, my thinness is caused by summer heat", I answered, bursting into tears' (Kigin).

'The birds, singing among flowers, laugh at men who have no leisure' (Sho-u).

Buddhism both the peculiar dash and fervour of Japanese fencing and the peculiar humility and quietness of the Japanese tea-ceremony, and explain that both were taught by Zen masters.

I wonder whether the calm and pacifism of the East is not, at least in part, to be referred to the benevolent teachings of Buddhism. Has any other Eastern creed, except Islam, ever taught the suppression of desire and passion, and universal kindness to man and beast alike?

The most widespread and the most efficient missionary enterprise ever sent out by any Christian church was undoubtedly the Society of Jesus. It was officially abolished at the end of the eighteenth century, and since its rehabilitation it has never been so boldly enterprising; but in its first two centuries it changed the history of the planet. It was the first world-wide missionary society, for its emissaries reached Japan going east and the Pacific coast of America going west. It was one of the most powerful educational forces the world has ever felt; it could educate a French nobleman, an Indian chief, a Chinese mandarin's son, and a Polish squire with the same tact and charm, toward approximately the same ends.

Two proofs of the effectiveness of the Jesuits as teachers: they nearly converted one of the most civilized communities in the world—the Chinese—and one of the least civilized— the Indians of central South America.

The story of their near-conversion of China is well known: they learned the language and then the arts and the poetry and the philosophy, and they entered China bit by bit, with infinite tact and caution, explaining always that they had come only in order to learn more of Chinese culture; they established themselves as scientists—primarily as astronomers, because the Chinese worried about the calendar—in the capital city, and set up an observatory; they merged with Chinese civilization so as to convert it slowly. One of them became a famous Chinese painter; one was tutor to the emperor. They were succeeding in Japan, too. They were overthrown largely by the intrigues of rival Catholic orders, not by the failure of their own educational technique, which has seldom been equalled. Good teachers are not always good diplomats.

Similarly in the South American lands which are now northern Argentina, Uruguay, and Paraguay, the Jesuits entered with the earliest settlers; they tamed the wild Indians, learning their languages, helping them to establish a more comfortable, orderly, and virtuous way of life; and then they set out to build up a civilization. They founded villages; explored unknown territories and mapped them; introduced efficient methods of agriculture and stock-raising; learned the languages and wrote grammars and dictionaries of them; botanized, discovering the hidden properties of plants; studied the weather, established observatories; taught the natives how to build houses and churches, how to carve, paint, and make music: a century later a traveller in Peru found the Indians still singing the songs and dancing the dances the Jesuits had taught them; organized their flock to resist the slave traders from Brazil, even forming a regular army and casting cannon. The ruins of the Jesuits' work still remain in a territory that has slipped backward since they left. It has apparently renounced education in favour of political and social independence, or isolation.

This whole question of the merging of cultures is sometimes complicated by sentimentality. I remember once being told by a student that missionary work was 'wrong' because it 'interfered' with the normal development of a people; or because it assumed that the persons sending out the missionaries were 'better' than those to whom the missions went. It is not the duty of the historian to make moral judgments of that kind. What we are doing is simply to discuss *what* happened, and to try to work out *how* it happened. But as private individuals, and as Christians, we can surely say that most missionary work has been beneficial when it has travelled from a higher culture to a lower, and that it is possible, even necessary, to assert the superiority of some practices to others. For instance, one of the most drastic changes made in any society by the irruption of new sets of ideas was surely the conversion of the Central and South American Indians to Christianity by the Spaniards and Portuguese. We shall be told that the conversion was not complete; that Indian Christianity still retains strong marks of paganism; that it was 'imposed' on the Indians; that it altered their 'true nature'; and so forth. But if we recall the hideous religion of the Mexicans, which involved human sacrifice on an enormous scale, with priests, who never washed off the blood of the victims, splitting open the breast of a young man with a stone knife and snatching out his living heart, and with the sacrifice of victims flayed alive to a god who was himself flayed, we shall not regret the change to a religion of peace and charity in which cruelty is a sin and not a positive virtue.

Let us now glance back over the further progress of this discussion. During this part of it, we have been considering the movement of ideas from one group to another as expressed in religion and art.

The first great example we chose was the movement of

Greek artistic ideas and techniques into the Indian and
Oriental world; we saw how the Buddhists were enabled,
by adapting these ideas, to gain a new conception of their
own religion, and how thereafter it spread throughout the
Far East.

A second instance, although it was a movement within
one culture rather than from one culture to another, was
the adoption of pagan symbolism in Christian art.

A third was the work of missionaries, and here we singled
out as specially effective and dramatic the work of Buddhist
and of Jesuit missionaries.

There are other channels we could have explored. We
might, for instance, study the use of translations to spread
ideas, and particularly the ideas of religion and of philosophy. The deep effect of the English Bible on British and
American thought; the enormous influence of Luther's
German Bible on German thought and poetry; the constant
activity of Chinese Buddhists in translating whole libraries
of Sanskrit works, and thereby enlarging their own language; the passage of Plato from Greek into Arabic, and from
Arabic into the Latin of western Europe—all these could
be discussed; and we could also point out that sometimes a
new translation, even if it be no better than the old, still
acts as a stimulus to new thinking about the subject . . . as
we notice with the new translations of the Bible today.

We could also have spent a profitable hour on a subject
we touched only briefly: the revival of Greek and Roman
art in modern art, beginning with the Renaissance, after an
oblivion lasting nearly a thousand years. We should have
pointed to the enormous impetus given to painting, sculpture, architecture, and interior decoration by the increasing
discovery and appreciation of Greek and Roman things—

from the fine Greek buildings of the southern United States to the graceful part-Greek churches of the North, from the Arc de Triomphe to the Madeleine, from the dome of St. Paul's to the Capitol, from the sculptures of Bernini to the paintings of Poussin, from David to Michaelangelo.

And perhaps something could have been said of travelling artists like the masons who built the medieval cathedrals, of men like Dürer, or 'Athenian' Stuart, whose visit to Athens in 1762 started the Greek Revival.

But we have outlined the essentials of this fascinating theme. Many artists are selfish, and many missionaries are wrong-headed, and many religious people are painfully limited. And yet, to us who are ordinary mortals, it is a constant blessing to watch the movement of the spirit of mankind, passing from one group to another in order to produce an easier or fuller appreciation of the beauty of this world, and a richer apprehension of the divine within us and above us.

RELIGION AND ART : BIBLIOGRAPHY

J. R. Allan, 'A Tabula Iliaca from Gandhâra', *Journal of Hellenic Studies* 66 (1946), 21-3.

L. Bachhofer, *Early Indian Sculpture,* Paris, 1929.

L. Binyon, 'Chinese Art and Buddhism', *Proceedings of the British Academy* 22 (1936), 157-75.

H. Buchthal, 'The Common Classical Sources of Buddhist and Christian Narrative Art', *Journal of the Royal Asiatic Society,* 1943, 137-48; 'The Western Aspects of Gandhâra Sculpture', *Proceedings of the British Academy.* 31 (1945), 151-76.

A. Coomaraswamy, *Buddha and the Gospel of Buddhism,* London, 1916.

C. E. Couling, *The Luminous Religion,* London, 1925.

H. Deydier, *Contribution à l'étude de l'art du Gandhâra,* Paris, 1950.

H. Focillon, *L'Art bouddhique,* Paris, 1921.

A. Foucher, *L'Art gréco-bouddhique du Gandhâra*, Paris, 1905-51; *The Beginnings of Buddhist Art*, tr. L. A. and F. W. Thomas, London, 1917.

G. Furlong, *Los Jesuitas y la Cultura Rioplatense*, Montevideo, 1933.

P. Gardner, 'Greek Influences on the Religious Art of North India', and A. A. Macdonell, 'Buddhist Religious Art', *Transactions of the Third International Congress for the History of Religions*, Vol. 2, Oxford, 1908, 79-85 and 74-9.

A. Grunwedel, *Buddhistische Kunst in Indien*, second edition, Berlin, 1919.

E. Hatch (ed. A. M. Fairbairn), *The Influence of Greek Ideas and Usages upon the Christian Church*, London, 1914.

A. von Le Coq, *Die Buddhistische Spätantike in Mittelasien* 1, Berlin, 1922.

M. Ricci, *China in the Sixteenth Century: The Journals of Matthew Ricci: 1583-1610*, translated by L. J. Gallagher, New York, 1953.

J. B. Pratt, *The Pilgrimage of Buddhism*, New York, 1928.

B. Rowland, 'Gandhâra and Late Antique Art: the Buddha Image', *American Journal of Archaeology* 46 (1942), 223-36; 'Gandhâra and Early Christian Art: Buddha Palliatus', id. 49 (1945), 445-8.

A. C. Soper, 'The Roman Style in Gandhâra', id. 55 (1951), 301f.

D. T. Suzuki, *Essays in Zen Buddhism*, 3rd Series, London, 1934.

M. Wheeler, 'Archaeology and the Transmission of Ideas', *Antiquity* 104 (1952), 180-92.

R. E. M. Wheeler, 'Romano-Buddhist Art: an Old Problem Restated', id. 23 (1949), 4f.

CHAPTER FOUR

Techniques and Ideals

DURING the earlier parts of these discussions, we have been thinking chiefly of non-material things—of plans for a national constitution, of methods of portraying a great religious figure, of poetic patterns, of types of religious activity. The movement of ideas can also be illustrated by the singular way in which new inventions travel across the world—new techniques in the use of material things. They, too, change history.

One such invention is paper. It was discovered in A.D. 105 by the Chinese Ts'ai Lun. Immediately it gave a tremendous impulse to the literature and culture of China. For some time it remained in the Far East. (Meanwhile the Greeks and Romans were using something less efficient, but cheaper and handier: papyrus, which is made of the pith of a water plant rather like the bamboo. Toward the end of the Roman Empire they gave it up and took to writing on prepared calf-skin, called vellum or parchment. Probably this change was made because the Arab invaders of Egypt wrecked the papyrus trade. Certainly one of the reasons medieval literature is so scanty is that it was written on vellum, a rare and expensive material.) Gradually, by another of those strange and almost unimaginable processes, paper began to reach the Western world from the Far East. About the year 700, an Arab garrison in the trading city of

Samarkand was attacked by a Chinese expeditionary force. The Arabs repelled the attack and took some prisoners. Among the captives were some Chinese papermarkers, who taught the trade to the Arabs. Thenceforth almost all Arabian literature was written on paper, and was therefore rich in variety and quantity. Paper took about three centuries more to reach Christian Europe. It landed in Sicily about 1100, in Spain about 1150; then it spread to Germany, to France, to Britain. Its effect on education and on all civilization since then has been enormous, and is not yet ended.

Sometimes we forget the most important inventions ever made by man. Surely these are cultivated crops. We eat hardly anything that is wild. Nearly all the vegetables, grains, fruits, and roots that we eat are domesticated. Somewhere, at some time, some inventor (or group of inventors) took a wild plant, ate it, found it good, and then discovered how to make it grow regularly. He improved its stock by careful selection. He put it to a number of different uses. No doubt the invention of cooking was made about the same time, for many plants are uneatable in their raw state, and have to be milled and baked, or boiled, or dried, or stewed.

Now, where were these inventions made? Where did cultivated plants come from?

There are only about a dozen centres from which cultivated plants originally came. They were invented there: from there they have spread over the rest of the world, changing human life as they went.

(1) The most important, and apparently the oldest, such centre of invention is the hills and lowlands of Central and Western China. No less than 136 edible plants originated

there, including tea; 14 different grains (varieties of millet and buckwheat); rhubarb, cherry, peach, apricot; many types of radishes and turnips (some Chinese radishes reach 36 pounds!); the 'Spanish' onion and the stem lettuce.

(2) Next in importance is India, the birthplace of 117 plants, including rice (which was later imported into China); sugar cane; oranges, lemons, mangos; cucumber and egg-plant; jute.

(3) Third, though still imperfectly explored, are the East Indies (including Java and the Philippines), which produced and tamed 55 plants, including the coconut palm, the banana and breadfruit, and many spices.

(4) Next is Central Asia, the high plateau (Northwest India, Kashmir, Tian-Shan, and Afghanistan), the home of 42 plants, including wheat (many varieties still grow there semi-wild); the grape; cotton; carrots, turnips, garlic; peas, lentils, beans, mustard, hemp.

(5) The first forage crops and the first orchards were invented in the Middle East, which has 38 plants to its credit, including the grape again; rye, as well as oats and several types of wheat; flax; alfalfa; the pumpkin and canta-loupe; the rose and the poppy; figs, pomegranates, pears.

(6) Next comes the Mediterranean world, the home of the olive, together with many vegetables and some forage crops. Here we find hops; leeks, beets, artichokes; varieties of grain such as spelt and 'Polish' wheat.

(7) Then there is Abyssinia, which had no fruit and no vegetables till the Europeans brought them in but which has an amazing variety of grains, 38 in all. It may be the original home of barley and of many wheat varieties.

(8) On this continent the chief centre is Central America, the home of maize; upland cotton (on which the world crop

is based); sweet potato; squash; cacao, sisal, henequen.

(9) Next come the highlands of Peru, Bolivia, Ecuador, which are full of endemic species, still not all developed. They produced tobacco; varieties of pumpkin; varieties of potato. (But the 'spud' or 'Irish' potato comes from the tiny offshore island of Chiloe, near Chile; it will fruit in long summer days, and the tubers from the Andes will not.)

(10) Last of all is Brazil and Paraguay, giving us peanuts, pineapples, and rubber.

Of 640 chief plants, over 500 belong to the Old World; and 400 of these belong to southern Asia. Few come from Africa, and hardly any from Australia. Of course varieties of great value may occur anywhere. Thus, the citrus fruits originated in southeast Asia; but the important orange called the navel first appeared as a 'sport' in Brazil.

Not all of them are of great importance: we could live without the onion; our lives would not stop if apricots were abolished; the peach is vital in Georgia but not in Vermont.[1] Yet wheat and rice and cotton and hemp and coconuts— large parts of our world are built upon them. An important social history has been written around the lowly potato. We might think that such inventions merely feed people's bodies and do not affect their minds; but consider the powerful effect of the Irish potato famine on the morale,

---

[1] Horace Walpole was once 'struck with the numerous ideas on commerce and civilization which may arise from a dinner', and said, 'Will you have a dessert from memory? The cherry and filbert are from Pontus, the citron from Media, the chestnut from Castana in Asia Minor, the peach and the walnut from Persia, the plum from Syria, the pomegranate from Cyprus, the quince from Cydon, the olive and fig from Greece, as are the best apples and pears, though also found wild in France and even here. The apricot is from Armenia.' (Quoted in *Table Talk*, ed. J. Thornton, London, Everyman's Library, 1934, p. 125.)

and therefore on the history, of the British Isles and the United States.

There are two important recent inventions which work directly upon men's minds, and which have circled the globe during our lifetime. These are motion pictures and the radio. The story of their development and distribution is well known. What will their effects be? We have heard optimists explaining that any such invention—because it makes communication easier—must assist democracy and increase enlightenment. But is that certain?

Radio is an invention as important as printing. People have been talking and listening for far longer than they have been reading and writing. People usually like talking and listening more than they like reading and writing. Most people in the world are illiterate or analphabetic, but they all like listening to stories and music. Also, reading and writing are largely individual enterprises: one man writes, and passes his thoughts to other men, who read his books separately and assimilate them individually. But listening is a communal activity. The vast communities of the illiterate world have always loved listening—to gossip, stories told by professional storytellers, poems recited by bards, sermons from holy men, and so forth. Now, through the radio, such communities can listen to voices of authority talking persuasively to them in their own languages. Because of this authority and because of this easy appeal to the communal audience, it is perfectly possible that the radio will spread not liberty but tyranny. If cheap radios are issued to a large population living in simple conditions and unable to read, and if these people are constantly exposed to the same line of propaganda through the incessantly talking radio, their minds may soon be conditioned to the placid acceptance of central authority.

Similarly, we believe that voting is a prerogative of the intelligent, and for us that means the literate. But in large areas of the world, anyone who can look at a symbol and make a mark on paper is eligible to vote. Now, what effect will the motion pictures have on such populations? Surely they will have the power to increase emotional excitement and to decrease rational reflection upon matters of social and political urgency. A picture (say the Chinese) is worth a thousand words, and there is no doubt that it is usually more exciting. Pictures that move and talk are even more emotionally stimulating. Powerful—I shall not call them ideas, but they are the roots of ideas—powerful attitudes and prejudices and stereotypes can be imprinted on the minds of huge masses of mankind by skilfully used moving pictures. In fact, as the use of radio and motion pictures spreads further, and as techniques of propaganda channelled through them improve we may expect to see the world becoming not more reasonable but more wildly excitable, pugnacious and pessimistic, madly revering and wildly hating, brave and frightened and seldom intelligent.

There are countless other examples of the spread of inventions and techniques, some of them unbelievably intricate. Take one small instance: the technique of bathing now found in clubs and hotels and gymnasiums, with steam rooms, massage, showers, and cold plunge. This is one of the oldest institutions in the Western world; and yet the Western world forgot it for a thousand years. It appears in Homer. From the later Greeks (like so much else) it was taken over by the Romans, and was developed to almost incredible grandeur and complexity. The great public baths in Rome were as colossal and as complicated as Radio City; Pennsylvania Station in New York is modelled on one *room* in the Baths of Caracalla. But when the barbarians arrived and the aqueducts were cut, such refinements were forgotten in the West. Christian ascetics were surrounded by the odour of sanctity; and the profane took gingerly dips into tiny tubs or steamed in primitive bath houses. In the Eastern empire, however, the technique of cleanliness through elaborate bathing establishments survived. When the Turks captured Byzantium, capital of the Eastern Empire, in 1453, they adopted the technique. Nearly three hundred years later, some Western traveller in Turkey saw and tried the baths; liked them; and, returning to England, introduced them there. They were soon established in various British cities, with masseurs, steam rooms, and all, often bearing the Arabic name of *Hammam,* and often called Turkish baths. But they are not Turkish. They are Greco-Roman: little do the patrons of the 'Turkish' baths in London realize that, as they lie steaming the chill out of their bones, they are only a few steps away from the remains of a Roman bath built by the Roman colonists in Britain—the bimillennial ancestor of their own establishment, revived after two thousand years of oblivion and discomfort.

TECHNIQUES AND IDEALS, AND CONCLUSION: BIBLIOGRAPHY

R. Beals, 'Acculturation', in A. L. Kroeber's *Anthropology Today,* Chicago, 1953, 621-41.

A. I. Hallowell, 'Sociopsychological Aspects of Acculturation', in *The Science of Man,* ed. R. Linton, New York, 1945, 171-200.

M. J. Herskovits, *Acculturation,* New York, 1938; 'The Processes of Cultural Change', in *The Science of Man,* ed. R. Linton, New York, 1945, 146-170.

Hu Shih, 'The Modernization of China and Japan', in *The Cultural Approach to History,* ed. C. F. Ware, New York, 1940, 243-51.

CHAPTER FIVE

Conclusion

IN these discussions we have been outlining an unusual approach to the study of history. We have suggested that it explains many problems which the standard histories treat less adequately. It is true that man is a being which loves power and fears oppression—so that much of his history is political; and man is an industrious and greedy being—so that much of his history is economic. But also, man differs from practically every other inhabitant of the earth in that he has brains, big brains, and enjoys using them. Our species is called Homo Sapiens; we have intelligence; and our history must also be written in terms of ideas.

Unusual though it be, this approach is not entirely new. If it were, we should have to distrust it a little. Various groups of scholars have been working toward it for some time.

Historians have recently been seeing more and more clearly that history is not only politics; that it is impossible to dissociate politics from religion, religion from social life, social life from literature and the arts, and in general to tear apart the strands that mingle to make the complex fabric of an entire culture. Some historians have written important books on individual cultures but have made the mistake of treating those cultures in isolation, as though each of them were composed only of people interacting with one another and with the physical environment: although in fact surrounding ideas and neighbouring peoples are a powerfully active part of the environment of many civilizations. This was one of the errors of Oswald Spengler. The mistake is not being repeated by Mr. Arnold Toynbee. The forthcoming ninth and tenth parts of his stately *Study of History* are concerned with 'contacts between civilizations' in space and in time; and although he deals principally with contacts involving violence or disruption—so much so that he occasionally sees interacting civilizations as 'assailant and victim' —he does also bring out the importance of peaceful and educative relationships between different cultures, and sketches certain 'laws of cultural-radiation' which explain these relationships in terms of his general theory of history.

Sociologists and psychologists have also been interested in the idea, not so much as a historical phenomenon but rather as a recurrent factor in contemporary life. Thus, they point out that it is not very useful to study a single Amerindian culture as though it existed by itself, in a vacuum. Most of the Amerindians were always colliding with one another, conquering or escaping or competing, adapting their lives to one another: it is impossible to understand the Hopi without knowing that they were constantly raided by the Navaho. Modern impacts are even more important. When one enters a Pueblo village which looks unchanged from the sixteenth century, when it was built; when one hears the old language spoken and sees the old pottery still being made, one will also notice an empty whisky bottle in a corner, and hear a Spanish-American dance tune coming out of a radio. The whisky was invented by the Celts; the glass, perhaps, by ancient Egyptians; the radio by western European and American scientists; and the dance tune by a descendant of the Spanish conquerors. All are now part of the Pueblo Indian culture.

The most determined attack on this problem has been made by the anthropologists. What we have called 'migration of ideas' they usually call 'acculturation' in this country and 'culture-contact' in Britain. Important work on it has been done by A. L. Kroeber of California; Melville Herskovits of Northwestern; Ralph Linton of Columbia and Yale; Robert Redfield of Chicago, and others. The student who is not an anthropologist may find their work brilliantly systematic but perhaps too closely limited to small and easily controlled problems, such as the interaction of primitive South Sea islanders and white men, but there can be no doubt that they have struck out many important lines of research.

The necessary first steps in studying this theme are to explain the concept, to demonstrate its importance, to select a few salient instances which will fire the imagination, and to sketch methods of future study. (From the anthropological point of view, this has been admirably done by Redfield, Linton, and Herskovits in a paper called 'Outline for the Study of Acculturation', dated 1936 and printed as an appendix to Herskovits' *Acculturation*.)

First, it will be necessary to define the subject, boldly, and broadly. This type of history studies the changes produced in one culture by factors introduced from another culture. It will not examine the growth of Greek philosophy or the development of the American presidency, because each was an almost wholly internal matter; but it will be interested in the workings of Greek philosophy within the Arabian civilization, or in the possibility that the 'balance of powers' on which the American governmental organization rests is really a Roman ideal formulated by the Greek philosopher-historian, Polybius, and imported into the

American colonies through eighteenth-century France.

Next, the anthropologists tell us we ought to distinguish ideas from things, material from non-material aspects of culture; and the historians and philosophers think we should distinguish techniques and ideals. Yet there will be many borderline cases. It was once said that material things could be taken over easily, non-material forms with great difficulty: thus, it was easy for a Red Indian to take to using horses instead of dogs as draft animals, but hard for him to give up his tribal organization. At present one of the chief problems confronting those interested in the Far East is to insure that Western ideals (the best of them) are transmitted to the Orientals together with Western technology. And yet there are difficulties here, too. The Chinese have often been more willing to accept spiritual innovations than to adopt new inventions, new methods of cooking or of tilling the soil.

Third, we must discuss the methods by which new ideas were introduced—by force, or by persuasion, or by mere attraction; over great distances of time and space, or by intimate contact, as with the Arabs and the Spaniards. Mr. Kroeber has pointed to one peculiar type of cultural change which he calls 'stimulus diffusion'. This occurs when someone in one group wishes to rival an activity practised by another group, and makes an effort almost independent of his own society. Thus, porcelain was invented, after considerable research, in eighteenth-century Europe, simply in order to equal and compete with the Chinese porcelain, which had been imported for two hundred years. The invention might never have been made but for that external stimulus. The same is true of the invention of the Cherokee written language by Sequoya. It is made up of letters that look like ours; but they represent syllables in the Cherokee language. He took the idea of writing from us, and he took the shapes of our Roman letters; and then he put the shapes to a different use, a use his own society would have taken many centuries to work out.

In this area some general principles soon emerge. One is that ideas can often be blotted out by force but cannot very easily and lastingly be taught by force. Another is that the most efficient way to destroy an idea or a set of ideas is to dislocate the social structure in which it lives, and then rebuild society on a different pattern, excluding the undesirable idea. Similarly, the best way to implant an idea is to assimilate it as far as possible to the host society, by making it part of the social structure, something to be learned by every child and accepted unquestioningly by every adult. Also, it should be taught not by visiting experts but by natives or by permanently established missionaries. Thus, the effect of British ideas in India is likely to be much more transient than the effect of Roman ideas in Gaul, because the Romans mingled with the Gauls, while the British scarcely mingled with the Indians.

Further, the student of the movement of ideas will have to judge personalities, asking who were the chief agents in introducing each new idea from outside, and who led from within in accepting it. We shall be surprised to find how few people it takes to influence a large society, provided their methods are efficient and their will-power is inflexible. The Jesuit missionaries who altered the history of the world were only a few dozen men; the leaders of the modern movement in Japan were only two or three hundred, but they moved mountains. It is for this reason that, when propaganda techniques are so well developed as they are today and when social and intellectual decisions are often swung by comparatively few men, large modern societies must be particularly wary of propagandists working either openly or under cover.

(The Chinese philosopher Hu Shih has asked why Japan was so successful in modernizing her country, while China was so unsuccessful; and he asks also why Japan, in spite of so much Westernization, has remained unaltered in spirit: witness the barbarities of her army and the primitive superstitions of her common people. He replies that it is because Japan has always been an authoritarian state, in which changes could be imposed from above and formally accepted, while China could be changed only by diffusion, since the Manchu imperial system had been destroyed. However, he asked and answered this question before the Communist revolution in China. We have now to see whether authority exercised from above and wielded by native leaders trained in foreign propaganda techniques will succeed in changing the Chinese, too.)

The historian who studies these matters will also have to estimate the importance and the effect of the innovations he is describing. Here again he will be prepared for a huge disproportion between the apparent importance and the ultimate effect of a novelty. For example, he will have to grapple with the fact that the Mexican drug peyotl became the basis of an important religious cult in the Indian tribes of the southwestern United States; that Arabian coffee was once a valuable stimulus to political activity in England; and that tobacco imported from America is now a vital factor in British psychology and, indeed, in British finance. If prepared for this disproportion (so that he will not expect to be able to establish 'laws' for many years), the historian will go on to examine how effective the various imported ideas may be. He will distinguish those that penetrated society by one entrance and never expanded from those that infiltrated at many levels and were widely accepted; he will mark out innovations that provoked opposition, brief or long-lived or passive or violent, from those that were accepted without trouble. And then he will try to discover why some were forgotten and in time abandoned while others moulded themselves into the society they had invaded.

Then again, the historian who works on these ideas must (as one of the anthropologists has said) use 'time as a dimension'. He must try to establish the exact moment when the external influence entered the culture he is studying, and the tempo in which it worked; how long it endured, and how long after it was withdrawn its later effects persisted. Often he will have to compare the present with the past. Such a comparison will not always flatter the present.

Take one easy, but often overlooked, instance from our own culture. Most of the greatest writers in the English language—and, for that matter, in French and Spanish and Italian and German, too—were trained in Latin and many of them were trained in Greek. Milton was a far better scholar than are most professors of the classics today. Shakespeare got more Latin at school than most modern youths get at college; and he went on reading the classics in translation and in the original throughout his creative life. Keats was not an untutored genius: he was a classically trained poet, and when he was still a schoolboy he wrote out his own prose translation of Vergil's *Aeneid*. Victor Hugo modelled himself partly on Vergil, partly on the satiric poet Juvenal. Walt Whitman's idea of delight was to ride on an open bus reading Homer aloud. T. S. Eliot knows many languages and has been president of the British Classical Association. Tennyson was able to recite Horace's lyric poems by heart before he was ten.

Now, some misguided educators, both in the United States and in a few other countries, believe that all change is necessarily progress, and that to abolish what is durable is a sure way to improve society. They have been doing their best to kill the study of Latin and Greek in schools and colleges—perhaps in an imperfectly thought-out reflex of resistance to the equally misguided old policy of making the classical languages compulsory. What will be the result?

We can see the effects of this activity already, in a painful lowering of literary standards during the past thirty years, despite the numerical extension of schools; in the rise of charlatanism in literature and in some fields of scholarship and educational technique; in the growth of the ridiculous idea that mental energy without training is enough to enable one to compose a play or make a speech or write a novel. Young scholars will undertake to teach Milton or write books on Chaucer without being able to read the books on which Milton and Chaucer fed throughout their lives. Men set themselves up as philosophers and argue with Plato and Aristotle without being able to read the writings of Plato and Aristotle and their contemporaries and successors. Half-educated showoffs acquire a reputation as learned men. And, worse than all that, the true standards for appreciating and understanding great books are gradually fading out of our minds, so that we believe they were meant only for amusement, hold that they ought to give up all their secrets in one reading, or else turn away from them altogether as 'not modern'. You will observe that all this is accompanied by a catastrophic rise in the incidence of social disorder and mental disturbance, because, the emptier people's minds are, the more easily they are thrown into chaos. You will have noticed also that literature is growing coarser and more violent, but is not producing books likely to survive; that most people, when asked about their reading, cannot mention anything beyond the novel, the short story, the film, the TV drama, and perhaps the book of popularized history; and that intellectual periodicals, which, in a smaller and poorer America about 1890, sold many scores of thousands, are now losing ground to large, vulgar, and simple-minded magazines full of intentionally crude pictures.

The historian of Western culture would be bound to take all these changes into account. If he were a classical scholar, he would be depressed. He might well foresee the coming of another Dark Age; or perhaps a Neon Age, full of comfort and gas and advertising and brittleness, not unlike the late Roman Empire. But he would take heart from the knowledge that such things have happened before without wrecking civilization—only stranding it (as it were) on shallow sandbanks until a fuller tide of tradition and creative thought rose to float it out again into the main current. He would see his work as similar to the magnificent achievement of men like Cassiodorus, who maintained the study and transmission of valuable books in his own Shangri-La while the world grew ever more barbarous outside his walls. He would recall the words of the founder of American literature and philosophy, Ralph Waldo Emerson, who said: '[Popular authors] may endure for a night, but Moses and Homer stand forever. There are not in the world at any one time more than a dozen persons who read and understand Plato—never enough to pay for an edition of his works;

yet to every generation these [works] come duly down, for the sake of those few persons, as if God brought them in his hand. The permanence of all books is fixed by no effort, friendly or hostile, but by their own specific gravity, or the intrinsic importance of their contents to the constant mind of man.'

These, you will say, are gloomy thoughts. They are. I do not believe that the classics and good literature are dying. But I am certain that they have suffered a series of determined attacks from people who profess themselves to be teachers, and that these attacks, as ruthless as they are ill judged, are continuing today. If and when the sciences are attacked with the same unscrupulous violence, it is probable that in a generation or two we shall have fewer scientists, and fewer of the comforts and deliverances from pain, fewer of the insights into the universe, which science confers on us. If music and art were being so relentlessly abused, we should shortly have nothing but hillbilly bands and comic strips and pretty-girl tobacco posters, as the successors of Bach and Rembrandt. Under the constant denigration of good literature—of course not only Greek and Latin but good literature in all languages, including our own—we may expect fewer and fewer good poets, playwrights, philosophers, storytellers, critics, and teachers to appear among us. One of my most admired colleagues, first my teacher and later my friend, once told me that he was convinced the aim of the educational revolutionaries was 'to make everyone else as ignorant as they are themselves'. Could that be true? If it were true, do you believe that they might possibly succeed?

In studying the movement of ideas, there is one further question, one of the most difficult of all. We must ask what the motives were which induced people to accept an unfamiliar idea. The psychologists and the sociologists have already worked out some of these. A very obvious one is fear. It was fear that their country would be invaded that caused some of the Japanese scholars to interest themselves in the organization and skills of the outside world. It was fear which recently led us to develop the applications of atomic fission. War, said Thucydides, is a violent teacher; but fear is a quick and efficient teacher. Human intelligence was developed largely through fear.

A second motive is pride, the desire for prestige. It seems that to have ideas originating outside one's own circle often demonstrates one's possession of a larger and more sensitive mind than one's fellows possess—like having foreign furniture or imported clothes. This motive may well be healthy, for some, if not all, societies are too limited; but it may also be mean and selfish even when its results are good.

A third motive is appetite, the desire for pleasure and comfort. Witness the way in which tobacco and chewing gum have spread all over the world; witness the drastic change in the habits of the crusading knights after they saw the luxurious costumes and furnishings of the Saracen officers.

There are other motives which the psychologists consider less important, and yet they also are effective. One of them is the interest in play: both active games and purposeless ingenuity, the play of the mind. Think how chess and golf and cards have spread all over the world; think also of the wanderings of marvel-tales and of decorative motifs both in clothing and in art.

Still more important, and more permanent than fear or pride or appetite, is the desire to learn, simply for its own sake: not in order to grow rich or to insure one's safety or to get more enjoyment from physical life, but simply to learn. Aristotle begins his *Metaphysics* with the words:

All men naturally desire knowledge.

And in spite of all our depression over the decline of culture and the abrasive effects of false educational theories, we may always console ourselves with that truth.

Let us look back over our discussions. We began by suggesting that history could be written in terms of the movement of ideas, as well as in political and economic terms. We exemplified that conception, in political and social life, by the history of great changes in Japan, Turkey, Rome, Spain, and Spanish-Indian America; and then, in religion and art, by the achievements of Greek artists interpreting Buddhist thought, Christian artists using pagan symbols, and missionaries both Buddhist and Jesuit: then we spoke of the profound effect of the movement of inventions from one country to another, using as examples paper, cultivated crops, motion pictures, and the radio.

In conclusion, we said that this way of looking at history was being worked out by historians, anthropologists, sociologists, and psychologists. We have been describing some of the ways in which the subject must be approached. They are not 'scientific'. They are merely logical; and with that logic must go the faculties of imagination and aesthetic appreciation, for men love power and have appetites, but they also have a taste for beauty and for the marvellous, and they have filled the world with wonders—not least through sharing the work of their minds with one another.

If now we accept this thesis, that history is partly made by the movement of ideas, we see what follows. It follows that a period of high civilization is one in which thoughts fly freely from mind to mind, from one country to another —yes, and from the past into the present. A barbarous epoch, a barbarous country, is one that attempts to paralyse communication, to keep ideas locked up, to treat thoughts as magic—either deliberately held away from the many or heedlessly scorned by the many. A sign of barbarism is the closed mind, which refuses to take in ideas from 'foreigners' and will not accept a thought derived from the past. Savages have narrow horizons. Civilized men see all round the planet and far into the past: perhaps even a little distance into the future.

The encouragement of this view of history is that it teaches us to hope. It shows us that it is hard to kill a good idea. A vital thought makes its way across deserts, through jungles, over oceans, between the barriers of language; it often survives the most fearful wars and devastations; it lies dormant but not dead for centuries, until it is revived; it forces its way past nearly every iron curtain, and spreads, multiplies, produces results unlike itself in quality and power. Jesus once compared the greatest of such ideas to 'a grain of mustard seed . . . which indeed is the least of all seeds: but when it is grown, it is the greatest among herbs, and becometh a tree, so that the birds of the air come and lodge in the branches thereof'. So it is with all good ideas. They outlive individuals—even the men and women who produce them; they outlive societies and creeds; they have a marvellous and unpredictable power to survive and to suffer change while retaining their vitality; and, when we trace the history of even one of them, it is easy to see why Reason has been called the attribute which man shares with God, the inextinguishable, the divine spark.